Gallery Books
Editor: Peter Fallon

A FAREWELL TO ENGLISH

Michael Hartnett

A
FAREWELL
TO
ENGLISH

Gallery Books

A Farewell to English
was published first
by The Gallery Press in 1975.
Enlarged edition 1978, reprinted 1991.

The Gallery Press
Loughcrew
Oldcastle
County Meath
Ireland

ISBN 0 902996 69 X

The Gallery Press receives financial assistance from An Chomhairle
Ealaíon / The Arts Council, Ireland.

Contents

for Bill Ambrose

Secular Prayers

1
to look at lovely things and not be dumb,
to cry and not be wordless, to praise
the relics, the remains,
the last insignia of God
in this,
the second mesozoic age.

2
whom I ask for no gift,
whom I thank for all things,
this is the morning.
night is gone, a dawn
comes up in birds and sounds of the city.
there will be light
to live by, things
to see: my eyes will lift
to where the sun in vermilion sits,
and I will love and have pity.

3
you are alive at last
to the discovery
of land, to know the ways
of cities and forget
the ways of birds. I wish
you grief in the concrete
galleries: but no grief
beside the cliffs of some
atlantic town, no grief
at nightfall to count stars:
only grief where man builds,
only grief in the city.

4
pray time for the man
from the soft inland:
(there is the sea, up
in parabolas
of foam, above the
rocks: the town in
nestling limestone under
wing, the smell of
the very cavities
of earth, a smell
of women, and cold
dead things) sea-sailor.

5
now the delicate
notes of wheat blow through
the harrowed earth,
this is the spring,
and so many flowers
walk the land in
resurrection,
and the filaments
of dead birds' bones
shine,
embossed like ivory
on the road.

6
I am glad for the frost,
leaves of exotic line
by ice on glass,
and trees made ghost
by flashes of light –
a bitter cold

from facets of icicle,
and crystalline
the animal tracks.

I am glad for the snow,
it is a white bird frantic,
a flight of white moths,
water frozen to intricacies:
and in the blinding neutral lull
all the ways made beautiful.
and for this animal wind
loose in the talking houses
I am glad, and in its will
bending the imperturbable,
the tree, the tower,
the turret of antiquity,
and quiet exhalations from birds' wings.

I am glad for the rain,
in its steel and distant parallels
on the square-cut leaf-thin
rectangles
the quarried slate on houses,
in its death-willingness,
its descent, its million
feet of birds across town houses.

for thunder, its talking on close days
is its prayer: pack ice calves,
there is a fall of rock:
it barks like dogs of god,
talks in tongues of fire:

deadly.
and electric.

and for the sun
will there ever be
an end of ceremony?
there is no more glory
hawkskilled eye can see
in the enterprise of night
the clouds of milk,
the silver bees,
than in a simple coming on of day.

7
hot the hanging apple,
the dusty bodies walk
the town, in neurotic
sweat: for summer I give
thanks. rivers are white with cool
and nothing sings: it is
the true gestation.
there is a flight of seeds
across an open place,
o hot the hanging apple.

8
'Amid the broken rocks
– shall we stay here
with the wild hawks?
– no, ere the hot noon come
dive we down – safe'
we will be here
with the wild hawks
when our intelligent
friend talks
to tell us of

his grief at ours.
we will not be safe.

9
I will love you
till your loving cease:
there will be no
more bargain in our lives.
we will not wear
the costumes of pretence:
you will love me
till my loving cease.
no act one, scene one
in our lives: you
will say the truth to me,
and not castrate
the brevity of love
in tense
neurotic silences.

10
there is surfeit of fungi
from the wet ground
in a moist luminosity
and a noise of pheasants
under fern:
fruit in scarlet complexes
on haw and dogrose:
toxic slime on fungus
stalks and the sleep-scented
pall of the autumn ash.
all things age,
all things are harvest
to themselves.

11
distance, and absence,
pares this oak of an
old remembrance down
to fragile lines of
nudity: there is
time, in guise of flesh
and long hair, there, by
me, now old from you
in new and eager
arms: but here, in new
and eager arms, I
do not shut you out.
I have loved you:
there is none more beautiful.

12
whom I ask for no gift,
whom I thank for all things,
down a tenuous dimension
I descend where all things
wild, the barking fox,
the wolf by grave, the ghosts
of dead, descend
and bodies longed for
in a fraction of the mind
are supine by wild ferns.
call here, wild eyes:
and I will wake
to the light to live by.
or will not wake,
but in a gentle trauma die.

13
black frost, pike locked
below the ice,
the winter season.
I give thanks for life
among these dead,
the bony men of trees
and the leaves along
the road, like the webbed
feet of dead
waterfowl:
the winter season,
the pike locked
below the ice.

14
what was not human
though from womb of woman,
for this a small grief.
for whom forced a love
on you, will have to be
the necessary funeral,
the necessary grief.
for you, already
skeletal, you have sinned
by forcing years of
faithfulness from us,
die now, rest: let us rest.
there will be valid
human grief for all
these deaths: the heart will love
all it has to love.

15
whom I ask for no gift,
whom I thank for all things,
there is a setting of the sun,
and a coming on of dark
and the familiar stars,
and the moon will run
crescent into clouds,
and all things but the night things
merge in their violent sleep.

16
o in this human city
there is only a human
season, concealed from my face,
hid frequency of birth,
the young in their concrete schools,
age forbidden to the flesh,
the dead in suburban cemeteries.
for me there are no seasons,
no coming of flower, or fall
of leaf: nor is there soft summer,
and the winter is mere rain,
and I adore them in their distance
for from the highest oblong house,
there is some intimation of the hills.

Prisoners

    brave
    to keep in capture
    whom he loved, this wild woman
    not so old, so many years
    in quiet place
    unknown to all the town.
so her face was white as almond
pale as wax for lack of sunlight
blue skin by her eyes in etchings,
all her beauty now attainted,
all her loveliness unwanted.
    not to say his love was lessened:
    no: he came home to her same altar
    at night, grey horse bore him to the threshold,
    quiet rooms, where the woman sang her service,
    sang to new gods, to the church of her invention
    her own cloistered psalms, in her bishoped dress of scarlet.
for she built walls to keep God in,
and waiting there from eyes ahide
at night before her tearful face
at calm crossroads her child did raise,
her child into the secret world.
    and she involved a secret Lord,
    prayed the holy prayers she made herself,
    and sang so: my Lord God is a human Lord,
    not Lord of towns, but Lord of white horses, holy
    of the hyacinth, the human Lord of light, of rain.
yes, Lord of sacred anguish, hear
me, and speak in rain of trees: send
your holy fire to heat me. I
cry: my Lord of holy pain, hear.
    house of slated roof was their house,
    daylight knew no way to hound them
            out of peace:

the door was closed with iron chains
locked safe inside an open moat
of water:
secret in their love they lived there:
the birch-hid dove was silk with peace.

The Retreat of Ita Cagney

for Liam Brady

1

Their barbarism did not assuage the grief:
their polished boots, their Sunday clothes,
the drone of hoarse melodeons.
The smoke was like the edge of blue scythes.
The downpour smell of overcoats
made the kitchen cry for air:
snuff lashed the nose like nettles
and the toothless praising of the dead
spun on like unoiled bellows.
She could not understand her grief:
the women who had washed his corpse
were now more intimate with him
than she had ever been.
She put a square of silk upon her head
and hidden in the collars of her coat
she felt her way along the whitewashed walls.
The road became a dim knife.
She had no plan
but instinct neighed around her
like a pulling horse.

2

Moulded to a wedge of jet
by the wet night, her black hair
showed one grey rib, like a fine
steel filing on a forge floor.
One deep line, cut by silent
days of hate in the expanse
of sallow skin above her brows,
dipped down to a tragic slant.
Her eyebrows were thin penlines
finely drawn on parchment sheets,

hair after miniscule hair
a linear masterpiece.
Triangles of minute gold
broke her open blue of eyes
that had looked on bespoke love
seeing only to despise.

Her long nose was almost bone
making her face too severe:
the tight and rose-edged nostrils
never belled into a flare.
A fine gold down above the
    upper lip did not maintain
its prettiness nor lower's swell
make it less a graph of pain.
Chin and jawline delicate,
neither weak nor skeletal:
bone in definite stern mould,
small and strong like a fox-skull.
Her throat showed no signs of age.
No sinews reinforced flesh
or gathered in clenched fistfuls
to pull skin to a lined mesh.

The rest was shapeless, in black woollen dress.

3
Door opened halving darkness bronze
and half an outlined man
filled half the bronze.
Lamplight whipped upright into gold
the hairs along his nose,
flowed coils of honey
around his head.

In the centre of his throat
clipped on his blue-striped shirt
a stud briefly pierced a thorn of light.
The male smell of the kitchen
engulfed her face,
odours of lost gristle
and grease along the wall:
her headscarf laughed a challenge,
its crimson wrinkles crackling.
He knuckled up the wooden latch
and closed the door for many years.

4
Great ceremony later causes pain:
next year in hatred and in grief, the vain
white dress, the bulging priest, the frantic dance,
the vowing and the sickening wishes, land
like careful hammers on a broken hand.
But in this house no sacred text was read.
He offered her some food: they went to bed,
his arm and side a helmet for her head.
This was no furtive country coupling: this
was the ultimate hello, kiss and kiss
exchanged and bodies introduced: their sin –
to choose so late a moment to begin,
while shamefaced chalice, pyx, ciborium
clanged their giltwrapped anger in the room.

5
The swollen leather creaks
like lost birds
and the edges of her shawl
fringe down into the dark
while glaciers of oilskins drip around her
and musical traces and chafing of harness

and tedious drumming of hooves on the gravel
make her labour pains become
the direct rebuke and pummel of the town.
Withdrawing from her pain
to the nightmare warmth
beneath her shawl
the secret meeting in the dark
becomes a public spectacle
and baleful sextons turn their heads
and sullen shadows mutter hate
and snarl and debate
and shout vague threats of hell.

The crossroads blink their headlamp warning
and break into a rainbow on the shining tar:
the new skull turns in its warm pain,
the new skull pushes towards its morning.

6
O my small and warm creature
with your gold hair and your skin
that smells of milk and apples,
I must always lock you in
where nothing much can happen.
But you will hate these few rooms,
for a dove is bound to come
with leaves and outdoor perfumes:
already the talons drum
a beckoning through the slates,
bringing from the people words
and messages of hate.
Soon the wingbeats of this bird
will whisper down in their dive:
I dread the coming of this dove
for its beak will be a knife

and if you leave armed with my love
they will tell you what you lack:
they will make you wear my life
like a hump upon your back.

7
. . . each footprint being green in the wet grass
in search of mushrooms like white moons of lime,
each hazel ooze of cowdung through the toes,
being warm, and slipping like a floor of silk . . .
but all the windows are in mourning here:
the giant eye gleams like a mucous hill.
She pictured cowslips, then his farmer's face,
and waited in a patient discontent.
A heel of mud fell from his garden boots
embossed with nails and white-hilt shoots of grass,
a hive of hayseeds in the woollen grooves
of meadow coats fell golden on the floor,
and apples with medallions of rust
englobed a thickening cider on the shelf:
and holly on the varnished frames bent in
and curved its catsharp fingernails of green.
The rooms became resplendent with these signs.

8
I will put purple crêpe and crimson crêpe
and white crêpe on the shelf
and watch the candles cry
o salutaris hostia.
I will light the oil lamp till it burns
like a scarlet apple
and watch the candlegrease
upon the ledges interweave
to ropes of ivory.

I have not insulted God:
I have insulted
crombie coats and lace mantillas
Sunday best and church collections
and they declare my life a sinful act:
not because it hurts
the God they say they love –
not because their sins are less –
but because my happiness
is not a public fact.

9
In rhythmic dance the neighbours move
outside the door: become dumb dolls
as venom breaks in strident fragments
on the glass: broken insults clatter
on the slates: the pack retreats,
the instruments of siege withdraw
and skulk into the foothills to regroup.
The houses nudge and mutter through the night
and wait intently for the keep to fall.
She guards her sleeping citizen
and paces the exhausting floor:
on the speaking avenue of stones
she hears the infantry of eyes advance.

Maiden Street

Full of stolen autumn apples
we watched the tinkers fight it out,
the cause, a woman or a horse.
Games came in their seasons,
horseshoes, bowling, cracking nuts,
Sceilg, marbles – frozen knuckled,
Bonfire Night, the skipping-rope
and small voices on the golden road
at this infant incantation:
   'There's a lady from the mountains
   Who she is I cannot tell,
   All she wants is gold and silver
   And a fine young gentleman'.

We could make epics with our coloured chalks
traced in simple rainbows on the road,
or hunt the dreaded crawfish in the weeds
sunk in galleons of glass and rust,
or make unknown incursions on a walk
killing tribes of ragworth that were yellow-browed:
we were such golden children, never to be dust
singing in the street alive and loud:
   'There's a lady from the mountains
   Who she is I cannot tell,
   All she wants is gold and silver
   And a fine young gentleman'.

Maiden Street Wake

I watched the hand
until a finger moved
and veins above the index knuckle
pulsed.
That was his last movement.
She had a band
of tan tobacco juice
upon her chin. Her few teeth buckled.
That was all the grief she showed.
In public.

Columned and black with women in shawls,
yellow and pillared with penny candles,
bright-eyed and blue-toed with children
in their summer sandals,
that was the mud house, talkative and lit.
In the bed, the breeding ground and cot,
he wore his best blouse
and would have seen
the finest teacups in his life.
But he was white
as an alabaster Christ
and cold to kiss.
We shuffled round and waited.
Our respects were paid.
And then we ate soft biscuits
and drank lemonade.

Epitaph for John Kelly, Blacksmith

Black clothes do not make mourners:
    the cries come out of the heart.
And local men at street corners,
    who have stood
    and watched grained wood
in horse-hearse and motor-hearse,
    white plumes of feathers, blue plumes
of smoke, to the dead man's part
    of town, to the rain-dumbed tombs,
go, talk his life, chapter and verse,
and of the dead say nothing but good.

    In Maiden Street
    what man will
    forget his iron anvil,
    an early Monday morning, sweet
    as money falling on the footpath flags?

Thirteen Sonnets

1

I have been stone, dust of space, sea and sphere:
flamed in the supernova before man
or manmade gods made claim to have shaped me.
I have always been, will always be: I
am a pinch of earth compressed in the span
of a snail-shell: galaxies' energy,
the centre of the sun, the arch of sky:
I became all that all things ever can.
I *will* be here: I have always been here.
Buddha had to walk upon me: my snows
were not so kind, my ice was sharp as grass.
Upon me, even Christ encountered fear:
the nails were mine, the mallet mine, the blows
were mine. *I* grew the tree that grew the Cross.

2
I am not free. I am bound by bread
to concrete chariots. My time is sold
for smallest coin, my acreage for beads.
The injury my freedom brings on heads
that are bound to me, that must always hold
on to me, because their essential needs
are love, and warmth, and bread, or seem to be,
is worth no walking on the mountains. Dread
is a bat ears never grow old to: sun
glorious on choral mornings can hear
it demand the insidious oarsman's fee.
I cannot go walk upon the mountain – run,
perhaps – but such a freedom, dogged by fear,
is just to be *one* guilt-edged morning free.

3

We can foretell the rising tide, the green
time of the wheat's nipple: we are not men.
Smiths, to your gold – carvers, to your agate.
We are men who are men, must not be seen
as men: make masks, make signs. Scribe, to your pen –
wonders, murders, myths and comets now relate.
The people's waiting eye begs for its hood
and will contemplate no magnitude.
The priest is the servant of blood: no gilt
or linen, or silver, or cloth of gold
can hide the true nature of sacrifice:
bread broke is bone broke, wine spilt is blood spilt,
bell is brazen gong. We, who once had souls
are now encased in pillared naves of ice.

4

Again, the coming round of time, the War
Of life become at last jeux d'Hecatombe:
The sudden herald of the blazing star
Into the piebald world will certain come.

After the twenty-seventh year, black popes
Will make an exile of the final Man,
Girded with satin, Satan and straw ropes
Flogged from the dungeons of the Vatican.

Who is this Christ, that he should challenge Paul?
What is this monster from the Middle Sea?
An invented state will have conquered all
And the Gentile feel the whips of Jewry.

With her vicious eyes slit in light, the cat
Expands like fungus in her habitat.

5

Something is blessed. I can tell my mind,
Show all the small parlours, all the wide rooms:
Façades much rebuilt on and hid behind
Dilapidated sheds and family tombs.

Something is blessed. I can sell my soul,
A guinea or a penn'orth: it resumes
Its place, and bargained for again is still whole.

Times it can be reckoned, if gold, in Troy –
Fine grains of love, filings of gentleness.
Or if sour black earth, in avoirdupois –
Whipping itself to hate when under stress.

The word is brain, made flesh to hold debate.
The very cells of hunger saying yes:
But the poem is the heart, incarnate.

6

Polyzoic demon, in truth thou art
Dark Asmodeus: teach me what I lack,
The secret of another human heart.

Teach me, the Circle of the Zodiac,
To scale the wall that keeps a man alone,
The method of compassionate attack:

Help me design *tormenta* that would stone
All the social ramparts round a mind
Or how to take the marrow from the bone

Or help me by some wise device to find
The soul's armour's single elusive crack
Or press me keys that silence will unbind—

Why I called demons with my magic rods?
I got no satisfaction from the gods.

7

A haphazard blue fire as Phoebus dies:
O sleep with Phoebus till the fight is won,
For he may die, but day will certain come.
What is this blue stone, kindred to the skies?
As ring of gold is brother to the sun,
As music of magic the gold bees hum.

With hunchback of dark the dead night defies,
Its silver eyes spy from their blackened lairs:

The soul hides in the womb and in the flesh,
Hides its terror in pleasure, safe a while
From the silkwhite, carnivorous mares
Which the pure unphysical minds enmesh
Who led by a holy angelic smile,
Turns from the body to the claws of bears.

8

Take this salve, Pamphila, oil of ages,
Pomade that eluded many sages –
Many half in love with sin and half with love,
Afraid to sacrifice a useless dove,
To sprinkle blood or to invert the Cross,
Afraid that any gain might be a loss.
Sweet Pamphila, all sacrifice is kin,
And Christ is used to catch the snake within:
Shapes in visitation to the crystal glass
Haunt the crypt and nave through the Pauline Mass.
Is blood of man, though God, more sweet in smell
Than spilt blood of a sinless cockerel?

Pamphila, take this salve: be brave, be bold –
All this knowledge for one piece of gold?

9
I saw magic on a green country road –
That old woman, a bag of sticks her load,

Blackly down to her thin feet a fringed shawl,
A rosary of bone on her horned hand,
A flight of curlews scribing by her head,
And ashtrees combing with their frills her hair.

Her eyes, wet sunken holes pierced by an awl,
Must have deciphered her adoring land:
And curlews, no longer lean birds, instead
Become ten scarlet comets in the air.

Some incantation from her canyoned mouth,
Irish, English, blew frost along the ground,
And even though the wind was from the South
The ashleaves froze without an ashleaf sound.

10

A soft internal music of his own
Played on his dead lips. His dead face was pale
And his dead eyes like almond-cuts in stone,
His nostrils gilt and sunk as Holy Grail.

And linen sheet and marble slab must bear
This fine body and black basaltic hair

A night in chapel and in father's house
Before the day and happy burial.
He was a soldier of the Golden Rose

And will embrace in earth the Holy Spouse
And end his sensual questing after all
In calm, erotic and profound repose.

He was a soldier of the Human War
For his few years, a perfect avatar.

11

To the vulgar speak only vulgar things:
For I have found the soul of this foul world:
God's breath lodged in a shell becomes impearled
And set into my sceptre and my rings.

I was the king of that ancient country
Who tried to embrace the Mother of God,
Bluerobed and gold, enamelled and moon beshod:
I am ash for my mad effrontery.

They give us demons to impregnate them,
But lust for Good must die inside the soul
Where mere angels are prostitutes unpriced.

So must I do with Mother Mary's hem
And die now, lost, but holy and unwhole,
Forbid to kiss the lips of Jesus Christ?

12
Here be the burnings, all for wizardry,
Done by the Bishop of Würzburg city:

The steward of the Senate, named Göring,
Senator Bannach, fattest man in town,
And Goebbels' child, a girl most beautiful:
Silberhans, a minstrel awandering,
And a blind girl whose skin was very brown,
And a student, new from the Music School.

Liebler's daughter: Madame Knertz: Schwartz a priest –
Nor was the innkeeper of Klingen released.
Valkenberger's little daughter, at home
Was executed, burnt outside her door:

Also some travellers going to Rome,
And Ehling a vicar, and many more.

13

Lamplight makes all trees circular, in streets
Where nymph and spirit never live and sing:
In Dublin town, this is a miracle.
Who has not seen this vision has no love,
Is surely urban as a house of glass –
The tree adore the sun within the lamp,
The tree attempt a dryad of its own.

Busy men build glaciers and the soul retreats,
Dies, as blackbarred wasps after their own sting,
In its small ivory winding of shell.
And weakly, velvet fist in velvet glove,
The heart is jammed at the vacant bypass
And trees conjure religion in the damp
In Dublin streets, cemented and alone.

Ssu K'ung T'u Walks in the Forest

A version of his twenty-four poems

for Liam Brady

1
The soul that rests has riches:
death in motion, bourgeois man.
I walked along the wood-track
with an old knapsack of truths,
by deserts and by spring wells
with an old knapsack of truths.

2
Quietness of the high flight
of the solitary crane,
of rustles of a silk robe,
of coveted sweetnesses,
of elusive bamboo flutes:
a thing we cannot pocket.

3
Gathering green watercress,
I saw a beautiful girl,
willows, peach-trees, orioles,
reality, and such things:
I embraced those infinite
and those ancient miracles.

4
The green pines in the clear air,
I take off my cap and walk
under branches of birds' song.
No wild geese in the clear air,
but through the moonlit barriers
I could converse with my love.

5

And the god with lotus hands
passed, to the neighbouring moon:
Mount Hua shouldering the dark
and bronze silence from its bell.
I saw a lunar halo
around his calm lotus hands.

6

In rain a gentle cleric
writing his flower-poems.
Hints of birds in the bamboo,
his lute in a green twilight.
In rain a gentle cleric
still as a chrysanthemum.

7

'Take the iron from your heart:
contemplate familiar stars,
do not underrate the moon
beam as a form of transport:
go back as light as child's steps
to your lunar yesterdays.

8

'Be vital as the rainbow
among the tall hills of Wu:
let the winds billow your silk:
keep Force as food in the soul:
create but do not grow less:
as the rainbow, give and live.

9
'If the mind has pearl inset,
what is gold to river mist,
to a branch of almond flowers,
to a painted bridge in mist,
to a friend at lute-music?
Simple things impearl the mind.

10
'Be wary of scrutiny,
of climbing mountains to look
down on birds, on waterfalls.
Do not climb up trees to see
a minute flower open.
Bow: it will be on the ground.

11
'All creation by your side,
the simple sun, moon and stars:
even a vagrant phoenix
and a tame leviathan.
God is not as far as Good:
open your palm, rain falls in.

12
'The poet can live outside
of print, but if his own song
cannot make him cry, if he
is not his first and finest
audience, then he merely
writes small words down on petals.

13

'That they might always come back
and be with us forever!
Bright river and bright parrot,
the stranger from the dark hill:
without the ash of writing,
may they always be with us!

14

'All words should be as things are:
artistic as flowers budding,
limpid as dew, important
as wide roads to horizons:
words should be as green as spring
as like moonlight as is snow.

15

'I sit here under the pines
reading the old poetry,
heeding only day and dark,
unaware of the seasons,
happy, poor and literate:
an old man waiting for God'.

16

Confronted by such repose,
my mind quits its tenement
and walks after its love: she
glides like a jade figurine,
her greenness into the glade,
becoming the glade with light.

17

I climbed the T'ai-Hsing mountain
and I made a small echo.
The trees were like seas of jade,
flower-scent almost opaque:
I heard it rebound from the
waterfall, the same echo.

18

With plain words for simple thoughts
did I not touch the heart of
Tao? For I saw a poet,
a man with sticks on his back,
a man listening to music,
and I had not searched for them.

19

She whom I asked will not come
and I am bitter as death.
Centuries die in the glade
and Tao is passing away:
whom shall we ask salvation?
Wind whistles, leaf falls, rain falls.

20

I held his image inside,
like the image of all waves,
of all green things, all blossoms,
all the barrenness of hills.
To have likeness without form,
is that to possess the man?

21

I plunged arm up to elbow
in a pile of damp green moss,
in broken tendrils almost
found it: and found it almost
listening to the oriole.
Elusive as a rainbow!

22

Never about to be grasped:
like the white crane of Mount Hou
like the white cloud of Mount Hua
like vigour in old portraits
of the armed ancient heroes:
just about to be disclosed.

23

Life can be a hundred years:
drinking wine from fine goblets,
talking with our oldest friends,
visiting flower-gardens
strolling with a staff of thorn
– but look at that great mountain!

24

I have made a simple song
walking now in the forest,
song of the Mighty Centre
– like pearls rolling on a floor?
– like turns of a water-wheel?
Explanations are for fools.

The Ruin that Befell Ireland

A translation of Aodhagán Ó Rathaille's 'An milleadh d'imig ar mhór-shleachtaibh na hÉireann'.

for Luke Kelly

My pity that Carthy's heirs are weaklings,
this poor land's people without a leader,
no man to free her, locked up and keyless
and shieldless now in this land of chieftains.
Land with no prince of her ancient people,
land made helpless from foreigners' beatings,
land stretched out beneath the feet of treason,
land chained down – it is the death of reason.
Land lonely, tortured, broken and beaten,
land sonless, manless, wifeless and weeping,
land lifeless, soulless, and without hearing,
land where the poor are only ill-treated.
Land without churches, massless and priestless,
land that the wolves have spitefully eaten,
land of misery and obedience
to tyrannous robbers, greedy and thieving.
Land that produces nothing of sweetness,
land so sunless, so starless and so streamless,
land stripped naked, left leafless and treeless,
land stripped naked by the English bleaters.
Land in anguish and drained of its heroes,
land for its children forever weeping,
a widow wounded, crying and keening,
humbled, degraded and torn to pieces.
The white of her cheeks is never tearless,
and her hair falls down in rainshowers gleaming,
blood from her eyes in torrents comes streaming
and black as coal is her appearance.
Her limbs they are shrunken, bound and bleeding,

around her waist is no satin weaving
but iron from Hades blackly gleaming
forged by henchmen who are Vulcan's demons.
Red pools are filled by her poor heart's bleeding
and dogs from Bristol lap it up greedily:
her body is being pulled to pieces
by Saxon curs with their bloody teeth full.
Rotten her boughs, her forests are leafless,
the frosts of heaven have killed her streams now,
the sunlight shines on her lands but weakly,
the fog of the forge is on her peaks now.
Her quarries, her mines, are exploited freely,
the rape of her trees is pointless, greedy:
her growing plants are all scattered seawards
to foreign countries to seek for freedom.
Griffin and Hedges, now upstart keepers
of the Earl's holdings – it is painful speaking:
Blarney, where only bold wolves are sleeping,
Rath Luirc is plundered, naked and fearful.
The Laune is taken without its fierceness,
Shannon and Maine and Liffey are bleeding,
Kingly Tara lacks the seed of Niall Dubh:
No Raighleann hero is alive and breathing.
O'Doherty is gone – and his people:
And O'Brien has joined the English cheaters.
Of the brave O'Rourke there is none speaking,
O'Donnell's fame has none to repeat it,
And all the Geraldines, they lie speechless,
And Walsh of the slender ships is needy.

Hear, O Trinity, my poor beseeching:
Take this sorrow from my broken people,
From the seed of Conn and Ir and Eíbhear:
Restore their lands to my broken people.

An Ceangal

They are my tormented sorrow,
  brave men broken by this rain,
And fat pirates in bed
  in the place of older tribes of fame,
And the tribe that has fled
  and who cared for poets' lives, defamed:
This great crime has me led
  shoeless, bare, through cold towns crying today.

Lament for Tadhg Cronin's Children

based on a poem by Aodhagán Ó Rathaille

That day the sails of the ship were torn
and a fog obscured the lawns.
In the whitewashed house the music stopped.
A spark jumped up at the gables
and the silk quilts on the bed caught fire.
They cry without tears –
their hearts cry –
for the three dead children.

Christ God neglect them not
nor leave them in the ground!

They were ears of corn!
They were apples!
They were three harpstrings!
And now their limbs lie underground
and the black beetle walks across their faces.
I, too, cry without tears –
my heart cries –
for the three dead children.

The Buffeting

for Healy and Broderick

1
What did I wake up to
but a bubbling trachea,
the drug inlaid upon my inner throat
like the roughest texture:
looked at the slim tobacco
in a rage and inlaid more.
I walked to the motorcar
and moved out through
a tedious range of colours.
Speed almost equals exhilaration:
but this is not the truth:
my organs, vessels, lungs
moved merely at a faster rate,
the tedious range of colours
merged more rapidly,
became an overlap of sights,
moved more rapidly to slowing down
to weariness, to total ruin.

2
And so the spectrum dwindled down
became a static and a separate
demonstration:
the puce, the black, the military grey.
Spittle seemed to reach
an unaccountable proportion,
the odour of cracks upon the glass,
the noise of many windows shattering.
I sat down there,
huddling my broken innards,
looking at points I barely focused on,

the puce, the black, the military grey,
miles from my face
too converse and in contrast
to be part of any harmony.
But I was here for some reason:
there was some meaning in this disintegration,
some old meaning.

3
I left the car.
The furthest points were colossi of sense:
my spine became erect
and lifted fistfuls of my softest parts
up and forward into some array.
But then the lungs snapped shut
commanded by some master sinew
and the heart became a ball of pain,
the target of some vicious nail:
and that buffeting began.
Eardrums toppled as if the air had fists:
breath was forced backwards by the blows:
head swung left: right: up: down:
like a frightened door:
heart noisily became a metronome.
Angry and insulting, I withdrew,
left the paltry habitat of the beast
and recovered in the clinic comfort
of the car.

4
That night
I crouched in a small alcove of heat
under a rough cloth rubbed hard
by years of limbs shivering,

recycling the same breath,
the same comforting smells,
I had escaped the bastinado.
But only for a while.
The sashes buckled
and the violent night
demanded entry: the drums
beseeched and screamed.
The gables cowered like a broken man:
and the pummeling insisted.
I screamed. I prayed to my forsaken gods.
But nothing stopped.
All night it fell upon the glass
like an angry couple
in another room.

Struts

We are all spread out upon a hill,
each to his ledge,
visibility almost nil,
seldom seeing each other –
hearing an occasional shout
above or below
and sometimes and most welcome,
seeing fires like silver spirals
jump along the crevices.
We are climbing upwards into time
and climbing backwards into tradition,
the sudden message on a rope
evoking the cosiness of soft-lit rooms,
the comfort and the smell
of sharing ancient overcoats.
Sometimes a rope gives,
implodes unweighted in the hand,
and then tradition, time and fire
mix in a spinning blur:
the hill unskins the knuckles.

Signal from the World

Miles, to the obscurity of some pelmet
cloth drags its oscillations.
Sitting here: for hours:
venturing sometimes to the concrete inclines:
sometimes climbing up
to where   is between me and the light
or dark or green blurs or white blurs
but not getting beyond it:
sometimes falling down the slope
but feeling no pain.
Just lying beside jute sacks among the grooves,
lying beside the giant flakes of paint.

Then there was that crack:
like a light bulb violently blowing.
And an undesignable shape
  – seemingly three-dimensional –
appeared between me and the light,
comparable to no familiar symbol.
It almost named itself.
But I could put no name on it.

Horse Breaking Loose

I was very young
and spirals of brown dust
broke into chaos on my sandals
and a long cone of white
tapered away to a line,
hot among dark edges,
walled by massive growths
of unfinished green.
At the apex of the cone
a figure like a smudge of rust
snapped into a violent smoke,
its black besoldiered
by a piping of black froth
and velvet pistons pounded into fear
and pieces of the road fell off
and fell disintegrating sparks.
All this violence and men running passed me by
with lashing whips of wire
and long outlandish coats
with voice and weapons most barbarous and uncouth.
I fell into a green and giving mass
and sweat performed a sickle on my face.

Early One Morning

There was nothing there
but the darkness and myself:
then slowly out of sleep
my eyes pulled me,
needled by a speck of lead dust.
No one else had thrust
a limb out of the headless
shadows of themselves:
I could see them stacked
on their beds.
At last I was the first.
A grey fingerprint
embossed my eye.
I knew I had something to say.
I began to cry.
A slow bubble of grey spread:
every shadow grew a head,
every shadow began to shout.
Then a film of blood
seemed to coat all things
and I was loudest of all beings
though my cry had lost its meaning.
A fan of silver
underglowed the blood:
we stared at each other,
none being understood
and grey and red and silver
washed the world
louder and more clear
than all our noise.

USA

They who were once proud of their persuasion
now in their declining jaws grow small bones,
their teeth grow huge, their skins turn yellow and
crack. They are slowly becoming Asian,
Apache arrows in their chromosomes.
They killed her lovers, expecting to replace
pure blood with their dubious bastard stocks,
using the weapons of civilized man:
bad alcohol and God, guns and small-pox.
Dogs with the right to bear arms would found
a juster republic.
                              Why are they afraid?
They live upon a burial ground:
Latin, Anglo-Saxon, Teuton, Celt and Jew
avert their eyes, afraid to look around
and see ghosts of Navaho, Cheyenne and Sioux.
They chained the land and pulled her down
and nailed her to the sea with towns.
She lies on her back, her belly cut in fields
of red and yellow earth. She does not yield,
she is not theirs. She does not love this race.
She will not open her legs to enclose
the scum of Europe, jockeying for grace.

The Oatwoman

She heard the gates of autumn
    splinter into ash
grey shock of toppling insects
    as the gate broke down.
Old nails in their nests of rust
    screamed at this swivel:
booted limbs of working men
    walked on her body.
Their coats lay down in sculpture,
    each with a tired dog:
thin blades quaked at blunt whetstones:
    purple barked at blue.
The whetstones drank their water
    and flayed the bright edge.
Each oat like sequin shivered:
    her gold body tensed,
fear lapped across her acre
    in a honey wave
and buckets of still porter
    turned to discs of black.
Iron and stone called warning
    to her shaking ears:
arms enforced a fierce caress,
    brown and blind and bronze.
Sickles drove her back and back
    to a golden wedge:
her hissing beads fell silent
    in dead yellow bands.
Across her waist the reaping
    whipped like silver moons,
wind whistled banked flute laments,
    musical sweat fell.
Animals left in terror
    pheasant, sparrow, hare

deserting her in anguish,
   crowding from her skirts.
She curled in a golden fear
   on the last headland,
the sad outline of her breasts
   bare through the oatstalks.
Four arms took sickles and swung –
   no single killer:
she vanished from the shorn field
   in that red autumn.

Pigkilling

Like a knife cutting a knife
his last plea for life
echoes joyfully in Camas.
An egg floats
like a navel
in the pickling-barrel:
before he sinks,
his smiling head
sees a delicate girl
up to her elbows
in a tub of blood
while the avalanche
of his offal steams
among the snapping dogs
and mud
and porksteaks
coil in basins
like bright snakes
and buckets of boiling water hiss
to soften his bristles
for the blade.
I kick his golden bladder
in the air.
It lands like a moon
among the damsons.
Like a knife cutting a knife
his last plea for life
echoes joyfully in Camas.

The Horsecatcher

Here was the river of our youth, browned by
bog in far-off uplands, the green hedges
crushing puffs of meadowsweet to the brink
of the water, the swallows overjoyed
at the new summer, the rats in silver
that swam across, the stoat in his waistcoat
eeled on the bank, and the stones were restless.
Pencilling their electric lines, plying
their blue wool, the kingfishers webbed the span:
the hooked trout jumped up; flicked his silver sickle.

Winkers and wet rope in hand, his hawk's eyes
blinking on their secrets, he left green footprints
in the white dew.
                    White horse, my holy anguish
tumbles like tambourines: it has no name.
Sin has no name in this townland: some men
have faults. Nested in green gloves, I slit the golden
throats of all the morning's dandelions,
and I wait in ambush.
                    Christ on His Cross
holds out no hope for me: Mary in blue
and gold will not crush me like the serpent.
I tell them over again. Forgive me
for what I am, but I am nothing else.
And the Church, inside, smells like unvarnished
boxes.
        Older than we are now and more
shrunken, not so brown and with fewer fish,
the river eats its red-earth banks like an
hourglass sand: it has uncovered a limestone
bed and cut a slow groove in the yellow mud
deeper than eels ever dreamed it could.

His body is there, Christ around his neck
for stone, his limbs white as water, his hawk's
eyes open on his secrets, soul at rest.

The Perpetual Moment

for Lara

I have looked into the jackdaws'
nest, ignoring their wild caws
to see a thing that always was.

I have looked at the pike's spiked jaws,
at the pads on foxes' paws,
to see a thing that always was.

I have looked at ice as it thaws
from the red beads of late haws
to see a thing that always was.

I have looked at fledglings' maws,
the delicacy of rats' claws,
to see a thing that always was.

I have looked for flaws
and found many: because
I am not content
to see a thing untouched
that always was.

Staghorn Whistle

for the Grahams

1

Man bundled in his frozen coats
cracked his fingers back to life
from his staghorn whistle
sucked a plug of ice
and shrilled a note.
I could see its blue parabola
drop where dog and sheep
smoked white in the grey air.

2

My uncle ran away from school
blue and free in a sailor suit:
the country heard his whistle blaring
pea berling in its spitfilled chamber.

3

I sit bewildered in machines
the lights and coils conveying
messages for morons
three inches of rough staghorn whistle
in my hand, a leaping frieze
of man and dog and mountain
my uncle dancing in the fields
and two gold girls in a morning stream.

The Possibility that has been Overlooked is the Future

I look along the valley of my gun.
An otter examines the air,
silver in the sun.
I have hunted him for many days.
I will not kill him where he stands:
double death in the breeches
demands he be given a chance.
I take stock, warm metal in my hands.
Will he swim upstream,
water from his nose a bright arrowhead?
Will he swim downstream
coiling in bubbles to the riverbed?
Will he swim cross-stream,
where an ashtree's roots are naked?
There is a chance he will swim towards me.
Will he take it?

Sallygap

It was left upon the granite cliff
like a discarded afterbirth:
not falling, at this distance
but like a fan of stiff
frost crashlanded.

It hung upon a cross of furze,
white like a waterfall,
moving, at this distance,
it meshes bleached,
like a lost scarf of lace.

Death by the Santry River

From her fabric bed the nylon sheets
cascade, gritting their electric teeth,
and fall on vinyl. The clock clicks alarm
and her irritated orloned arm
reaches for a switch. Her feet slip in
to nylon, puffed and feminine:
she sips a liquid vitamin.
She sparks an orlon nightdress to the floor:
chemical solutions clean her pores.
She dons more nylon, does her hair,
fixing down each segment with a spray,
non-toxic, not to be exposed to flame.
She leaves with plastic bag and shoes
the safety of her airconditioned mews
and taps a plastic sound
across uncultivated ground

for green bracelets,
bindweed tendrils mongreled at her heels,
like bronzed bracelets greened by rain:
briars bounded in green loops,
lust on their thorntips:
white bugles blew obscene advance,
tendrils pulled her down
and grasses stabbed:
quivers of rush enter her wet mouth,
needling through the red muscle of her cheeks:
she's down:
a broken heel sticks dead
a black mushroom in the mud
swiftly to every orifice goosegrass claws
an avalanche of burrs descends her neck
burdock leech her throat like puffs of pain
hawthorn javelins poise in ranks

uncurling fernheads push aside her nipples
thistles explode inside her womb
red syllables of froth bloom from her lips:
she dies in shrouds of thistledown,
wrapped in this violent jewelry.

Dryad

Walking in our public places,
seeing the latest art
made from the latest materials
is like finding words like 'dryad'
shattered from their plinths,
statues without squares
broken marble heads of beasts:
commas of culture left
and culture lost in this city of the warehouse.

Here is a figure in metallic foil
its forty-three filaments or coils
in a perpetual tremble.
Not beautiful, not useful
but the image was the maker's own:
perhaps he heard his soul
crying outside our ramparts
or honking at a vacant by-pass.

When our neon lights drop bluely
from the warehouse windowglass
and smoky rain sneaks down the walls
the figure in metallic foil
attempts a dryad of its own
takes the time-encrusted light
as its central soul
from which the broken circles spin.

Who cannot see this vision has no love –
    dryad
    and her attendant ghosts
    caught in the pointless barbs
    of the metallic foil.

The Final Rendezvous

Black frost hammered the ground hard
cutting graveyard trees to shapes
of flat tin, studding the thorns
with spurs and horns of white grace.
Prongs of grass with iron root
snapped underfoot like small bones
and a white smoke of grief bound
mourners in an owl-soft tone.
Lovely, presenting a pale
face, pallor of ship and train,
her daughter and my love
watched the shovel-handle break
as obstinate ground made room,
(toppling eardrums full of sea,
and unpolished-plum-dull eyes
searching for a sullen grief).
She saw me, and saw, before
heart's door opened up in pain,
love-sending eyes: then she knew
her true emotion was rage.
Ice fell as the yew's spine snapped.
Ice fell as the yew's spine snapped.

Theory

for Rosemary

By glass engraved with Rousseau jungles
by frost and its momentary ferns
an old music from some other place
runs, like milk on marble tables –
a phrasing from the stellar sound,
the pure monoword:
one poem writing a book of poets.
And when this sound becomes emotion
that is the moment when the god descends.
And when the clever trap of style
snaps through the costume
it brings out the bone,
the image no mirror ever brings to bay,
the single syllable explosion.
When this emotion becomes sound
that is the moment when the god descends.

A Visit to Castletown House

for Norah Graham

The avenue was green and long, and green
light pooled under the fernheads; a jade screen
could not let such liquid light in, a sea
at its greenest self could not pretend to be
so emerald. Men had made this landscape
from a mere secreting wood: knuckles bled
and bones broke to make this awning drape
a fitting silk upon its owner's head.

The house was lifted by two pillared wings
out of its bulk of solid chisellings
and flashed across the chestnut-marshalled lawn
a few lit windows on a bullock bawn.
The one-way windows of the empty rooms
reflected meadows, now the haunt
of waterbirds: where hawtrees were in bloom,
and belladonna, a poisonous plant.

A newer gentry in their quaint attire
looked at maps depicting alien shire
and city, town and fort: they were his seed,
that native who had taken coloured beads
disguised as chandeliers of vulgar glass
and made a room to suit a tasteless man
– a graceful art come to a sorry pass –
painted like some demented tinker's van.

But the music that was played in there –
that had grace, a nervous grace laid bare,
Tortelier unravelling sonatas
pummelling the instrument that has

the deep luxurious sensual sound,
allowing it no richness, making stars
where moons would be, choosing to expound
music as passionate as guitars.

I went into the calmer, gentler hall
in the wineglassed, chattering interval:
there was the smell of rose and woodsmoke there.
I stepped into the gentler evening air
and saw black figures dancing on the lawn,
Eviction, Droit de Seigneur, Broken Bones:
and heard the crack of ligaments being torn
and smelled the clinging blood upon the stones.

Mrs Halpin and the Lightning

When thunder entered like an Easter priest
and draped its purple on Mullach a' Radhairc
a horse took fright and broke its neck
against a pierstone:
the carshafts gave like small bones
and the tilted wheel spun.
When the blue sheets crackled
with electric starch
Mrs Halpin with a goose's wing
flailed holy water drops
like the steel tips of holy whips
to beat the demons from the room.
But they would not go away.
Their garments shook her rosary
as they danced on the stone floor.
Her fear was not the simple fear of one
who does not know the source of thunder:
these were the ancient Irish gods
she had deserted for the sake of Christ.
They waited in the earth and sky
to punish and destroy
their fickle congregation.
Mrs Halpin knew the reason why.

Death of an Irishwoman

Ignorant, in the sense
she ate monotonous food
and thought the world was flat,
and pagan, in the sense
she knew the things that moved
at night were neither dogs nor cats
but *púcas* and darkfaced men,
she nevertheless had fierce pride.
But sentenced in the end
to eat thin diminishing porridge
in a stone-cold kitchen
she clenched her brittle hands
around a world
she could not understand.
I loved her from the day she died.
She was a summer dance at the crossroads.
She was a cardgame where a nose was broken.
She was a song that nobody sings.
She was a house ransacked by soldiers.
She was a language seldom spoken.
She was a child's purse, full of useless things.

A Visit to Croom 1745

for Séamus O Cinnéide

The thatch dripped soot,
the sun was silver
because the sky
from ruts of mud to high blaze
was water:
whitewashed walls were silver,
limeflakes opened like scissored pages
nesting moss and golds of straw
and russet pools of soot:
windows small as rat holes
shone like frost-filled hoofprints,
the door was charted
by the tracery of vermin.
Five Gaelic faces stopped their talk,
turned from the red of fire
into a cloud of rush-light fumes,
scraped their pewter mugs
across the board and talked about the king.
I had walked a long time
in the mud to hear
an avalanche of turf fall down,
fourteen miles in straw-roped overcoat
passing for Irish all along the road
now to hear a Gaelic court
talk broken English of an English king.
It was a long way
to come for nothing.

A Farewell to English

for Brendan Kennelly

1

Her eyes were coins of porter and her West
Limerick voice talked velvet in the house:
her hair was black as the glossy fireplace
wearing with grace her Sunday-night-dance best.
She cut the froth from glasses with a knife
and hammered golden whiskies on the bar
and her mountainy body tripped the gentle
mechanism of verse: the minute interlock
of word and word began, the rhythm formed.
I sunk my hands into tradition
sifting the centuries for words. This quiet
excitement was not new: emotion challenged me
to make it sayable. The clichés came
at first, like matchsticks snapping from the world
of work: *mánla, séimh, dubhfholtach, álainn, caoin:*
they came like grey slabs of slate breaking from
an ancient quarry, *mánla, séimh, dubhfholtach,*
álainn, caoin, slowly vaulting down the dark
unused escarpments, *mánla, séimh, dubhfholtach,*
álainn, caoin, crashing on the cogs, splinters
like axeheads damaging the wheels, clogging
the intricate machine, *mánla, séimh,*
dubhfholtach, álainn, caoin. Then Pegasus
pulled up, the girth broke and I was flung back
on the gravel of Anglo-Saxon.
What was I doing with these foreign words?
I, the polisher of the complex clause,
wizard of grasses and warlock of birds,
midnight-oiled in the metric laws?

2

Half afraid to break a promise
made to Dinny Halpin Friday night
I sat down from my walk to Camas
Sunday evening, Doody's Cross,
and took off my burning boots
on a gentle bench of grass.
The cows had crushed the evening
green with mint.
Springwater from the roots
of a hawkfaced firtree on my right
swamped pismires bringing home
their sweet supplies
and strawberries looked out
with ferrets' eyes.
These old men walked on the summer road
sugán belts and long black coats
with big ashplants and half-sacks
of rags and bacon on their backs.
They stopped before me with a knowing look
hungry, snotnosed, half-drunk.
I said 'grand evening',
and they looked at me a while
then took their roads
to Croom, Meentogues and Cahirmoyle.
They look back once,
black moons of misery
sickling their eye-sockets,
a thousand years of history
in their pockets.

3

Chef Yeats, that master of the use of herbs
could raise mere stew to a glorious height,
pinch of saga, soupçon of philosophy
carefully stirred in to get the flavour right,
and cook a poem around the basic verbs.
Our commis-chefs attend and learn the trade,
bemoan the scraps of Gaelic that they know:
add to a simple Anglo-Saxon stock
Cuchulainn's marrow-bones to marinate,
a dash of Ó Rathaille simmered slow,
a glass of University hic-haec-hoc:
sniff and stand back and proudly offer you
the celebrated Anglo-Irish stew.

4

We woke one morning
in a Dublin digs
and found we were descended
from two pigs.
The brimming Irish sow
who would allow
any syphilitic boar
to make her hind-end sore
was Mammy.
Daddy was an English boar
who wanted nothing
but
a sweaty rut
and ownership of any offspring.
We knew we had been robbed
but were not sure that we lost
the right to have a language
or the right to be the boss.

So we queued up at the Castle
in nineteen-twenty-two
to make our Gaelic
or our Irish dream come true.
We could have had from that start
made certain of our fate
but we chose to learn the noble art
of writing forms in triplicate.
With big wide eyes
and childish smiles
quivering on our lips
we entered the Irish paradise
of files and paper-clips.

5

I say farewell to English verse,
to those I found in English nets:
my Lorca holding out his arms
to love the beauty of his bullets,
Pasternak who outlived Stalin
and died because of lesser beasts:
to all the poets I have loved
from Wyatt to Robert Browning:
to Father Hopkins in his crowded grave
and to our bugbear Mr Yeats
who forced us into exile
on islands of bad verse.

Among my living friends
there is no poet I do not love,
although some write
with bitterness in their hearts:
they are one art, our many arts.

Poets with progress
make no peace or pact:
the act of poetry
is a rebel act.

6

Gaelic is the conscience of our leaders,
the memory of a mother-rape they will
not face, the heap of bloody rags they see
and scream at in their boardrooms of mock oak.
They push us towards the world of total work,
our politicians with their seedy minds
and dubious labels, Communist or
Capitalist, none wanting freedom –
only power. All that remind us
we are human and therefore not a herd
must be concealed or killed or slowly left
to die, or microfilmed to waste no space.
For Gaelic is our final sign that
we are human, therefore not a herd.

I saw our governments the other night –
I think the scene was Leopardstown –
horribly deformed dwarfs rode the racetrack
each mounted on a horribly deformed dwarf:
greenfaced, screaming, yellow-toothed, prodding
each other with electric prods, thrashing
each others' skinny arses, dribbling snot
and smeared with their own dung, they galloped
towards the prize, a glass and concrete anus.

I think the result was a dead heat.

7

This road is not new.
I am not a maker of new things.
I cannot hew
out of the vacuumcleaner minds
the sense of serving dead kings.

I am nothing new
I am not a lonely mouth
trying to chew
a niche for culture
in the clergy-cluttered south.

But I will not see
great men go down
who walked in rags
from town to town
finding English a necessary sin
the perfect language to sell pigs in.

I have made my choice
and leave with little weeping:
I have come with meagre voice
to court the language of my people.

Notes

Page 61   Camas: a townland five miles south of Newcastle West in Co. Limerick where I spent most of my childhood.

75   Mullach a' Radhairc: hills to the south-west of Newcastle West.

78   *dubhfholtach:* blacklocked. *álainn:* beautiful. *mánla, séimh* and *caoin:* words whose meanings hover about the English adjectives graceful, gentle.

79   Croom: area in Co. Limerick associated with Andrias Mac Craith (d. 1795); also, seat of the last 'courts' of Gaelic poetry; also, my birthplace.

Meentogues: birthplace of Aodhagán Ó Rathaille.

Cahirmoyle: site of the house of John Bourke (fl. 1690), patron of Dáibhí Ó Bruadair.

Contents

Introduction

This book combines some of the more unusual crimes to have occurred within the County with titbits of local history, parade room gossip and folklore tales which country 'bobbies' have a flair for unearthing from local sources. Some of the murders described are now ancient history but others quite recent. It is not only crime, however, which sticks in the memories of country folk. There are stories handed down through the ages of evil deeds and spirits which cannot rest. Even today there are certain places where the locals will not tread after dark.

The book also provides an insight into what early policing was like and shows that some of our towns were not always as peaceful or law-abiding as they are today. A number of mysteries still remain unexplained and some murders, as yet, unsolved.

The reader should bear in mind, however, that most country tales are passed down by word of mouth and that with passage of time variations will occur. Many will have been recorded in writing and published elsewhere over the years so to that extent the contents cannot claim to be unique although stories based on certain personal recollections are published for the first time.

It is also pointed out that, within the context of the title, Devon does not include the cities of Exeter or Plymouth apart from the odd fleeting references. Both were outside of the area policed by the Devon Constabulary until the amalgamation of Forces in 1966 and 1967. In covering the County the reader will basically follow the route taken during the author's career as he moved from area to area. It is not his personal story but one about Devon's characters, the good and the bad, and those occurrences which fascinate not only policemen but very many others.

It is, therefore, neither a tourist guide nor history book but a mixture of both which it is hoped will give the reader a view of Devon in a way which has not been attempted before. If, by the time the last page is reached, the reader knows a little more about the County than when he, or she, started then the author will have achieved his goal.

The peaceful village of Whimple where a foul murder was commited

Branscombe Church, burial place of an unfortunate exciseman who died in suspicious circumstances in 1755

Chapter 1
East Devon

Exmouth: *Bread Riots and Boats*

Woodbury Common: *Adders and Arson?*

Budleigh Salterton: *Millais and Murder*

East Budleigh: *The Smuggling Vicar*

Otterton: *The French Connection*

Sidmouth: *Folk Music & The Sainsbury Case*

Salcombe Regis: *The Body Snatchers*

Branscombe & Beer: *Smuggling Country & The Excise Man*

Loughwood: *Chapel Hidden From The Law*

Yarcombe: *The Constabulary's Last Outpost*

Dunkeswell: *The Magna Carta & Kennedy Connections*

Culmstock: *The Case Of The Drunken Woman*

Clayhidon: *The Murdered Surveyor*

Honiton: *The Salvation Army Riots*

Ottery St Mary: *Tar Barrels and Blunderbuses*

Whimple: *The Murder Of P.C. Potter*

Aylesbeare: *The Genette Tate Mystery*

I start the journey through Devon in the east of the County and at Exmouth in particular. This area has always occupied a special place in my life because not only was I brought up here but this is where, on leaving school in 1949, I joined the Devon Constabulary as a Police Cadet. It was then that I began to see East Devon in a completely new light. I already knew a little of local history but tales of smuggling and other yarns, such as the resurrection corkscrew, gripped the imagination and I was eager to learn more. This local knowledge was even further enhanced when I returned to the town in 1966 as Sergeant in Charge of the East Devon Traffic Section and my area of responsibility stretched as far as the Dorset boundary.

Exmouth
From Bread Riots to Boats

Exmouth's old red brick police station still stands in Victoria Road although it was converted some years ago into the town's Working Men's Club. Commissioned in 1914, it was Exmouth's third Police Station. The original 'clink' was destroyed in 1866 when progress dictated it made way for the cutting of the new Rolle Street. Alternative premises were found in South Street until the move to Victoria Road at the outbreak of the first World War.

At this time the police station was the most important in the area with status as a Divisional Headquarters and a lay-out typical of the era. Immediately inside the front door of the building was the charge-room, complete with tall wooden desk and cord operated telephone exchange. To the rear was a stone passage containing half-a-dozen cells, each with bare board bed, and a prisoners' exercise yard. One of the more unsavoury tasks to befall the young cadets was to 'swill out' after the overnight cider drinkers had appeared before the local magistrates. It was a short journey; the local court connected to the police station on the Imperial Road side of the building and can be easily recognised today. The row of first floor windows overlooking Victoria Road belonged to the single men's quarters and in those days it was a disciplinary offence to move outside the town without a leave pass. Somehow today's modern complex in North Street seems to lack the authoritative appearance of the old building which sadly became too small for current needs in the nineteen seventies.

Wherever one travels in Devon the sea is never far away and the County's maritime heritage is second to none. Exmouth, for its part, boasts the fact that it is the County's oldest resort and with a two mile promenade has one of the finest stretches of sand to be found on the County's southern coast. The fine terrace of Georgian houses along The Beacon, overlooking both the sea and estuary, bear witness to its grandeur in days gone by. No.6 was the home of the forlorn wife of Lord Nelson for over a quarter of a century and her remains now lay interred on the outskirts of town in the cemetery of Littleham Parish Church. The grave lies in the lower corner near the road and under a large yew tree. Her near neighbour on the Beacon was Lady Byron, wife of the celebrated poet, who lived with her daughter Ada for a short period at No.19, now appropriately known as Byron Court.

Also buried in Littleham cemetery are the remains of 'Old Isaac Rake' who was Exmouth's Peace Office in the first half of the nineteenth century. Before coming to Exmouth he had been a Constable in London and had been on duty at the coronation of Queen Victoria. If on coming to Exmouth in 1842, and taking the appointment of Parish Constable, he thought he would have a quiet time then it appears he was mistaken. One of the town's sporting pursuits he quickly brought tot a close after his arrival was the illegal cock-fighting which was a regular occurrence in what are now the Manor Gardens.

He was still serving as Parish Constable when Bread Riots

started on November 5th 1867. During the course of the night the crowd rampaged through the streets of Exmouth smashing shop windows and doors as they went. Isaac Rake went out to tackle them only to be faced by the mob retreating at speed down Boarden Barn at the top of Fore Street. As they fled towards him one shouted a warning to the effect that the farmer up the road had turned loose his bull. That, at least, was a novel way of stopping the progress of a rampaging mob!

It was during these riots that the flour and corn mill in Withycombe Village Road came under attack and was stoned by the mob. A sluice gate controlled its source of water from the Withy Brook. But such is fate, having survived the ravages of man it was to fall almost a century later to the forces of nature. In 1960 severe storms caused the brook to overflow and the spate of water not only destroyed the mill but put most of the town under several feet of water. Fortunately, flood prevention schemes constructed as a result have ensured the town enjoyed a dry future. The water wheel from the old mill was subsequently re-sited at the commencement of Madeira Walk and in its present scenic location, surrounded by flowers, gives the passer-by little idea of its more turbulent past.

Exmouth has long played host to the Armed Forces, particularly the Royal Marines. Their war-time camp at Dalditch, on the fringe of Woodbury Common, disappeared years ago but today, a few miles away at Lympstone, is the modern home of the Royal Marines Commando Training Centre. The self-discipline of the Corps is such that rarely are the local police caused any real problems, with minor misdemeanours quickly and more severely dealt with by the camp authorities themselves. But it appears Exmouth was not always so lucky. In the summer of 1893 there was serious trouble in the town when a large number of troops from the battalions of the Royal Welsh Regiment and South Wales Borderers broke from their camp on Woodbury Common. Their behaviour gave rise to a complaint from a member of the public, and as a result one of the soldiers was arrested and struggled violently all the way to the police station. His colleagues were then joined by some of the more unruly townsfolk and attacked the police station which had to be barricaded. Only the arrival of a military picket prevented successful use of a battering ram but nevertheless a lot of damage was caused. Although more arrests were made the trouble moved from Exmouth to Woodbury where damage was caused to shops and the village pub. Looking at Woodbury today it seems hard to believe that in 1878 there was a police contingent in the village which warranted a Sergeant 1st Class in charge.

During World War II, in keeping with most of the South Coast, Exmouth saw its share of military activity. The Maer, today a favourite spot for ball games behind the Esplanade, and home to the town's cricket club, became a large U.S. Army camp when it was commandeered from the local golf club. Heavy artillery was embedded in the side of the cliffs at the Orcombe Point end of the sea front, the barrels of the large guns pointed seawards towards the potential enemy. The harbour was a base for a sleek R.A.F. Air Sea Rescue craft which were kept at a moment's readiness to go to the aid of allied fliers who were forced to ditch in the sea.

After the war it was this same harbour which was to become a major source of income for the town. Unfortunately the once thriving port is now closed with plans to turn it into a fashionable marina. It is hard to visualise that it used to be packed with freighters of up to a thousand tonnes carrying a variety of cargoes, from timber and coal to animal feed and fertilisers. Ships came from all over Europe, including the former iron-curtain countries, and over the years local police officers kept in readiness plans for dealing with the occasional requests for political asylum! The docks were also an area of danger for the unwary and many's the time when drunken seamen have been fished out of its waters ... and not always alive.

On some occasions the death was not accidental ... but murder. One such crime, before the docks were closed to shipping, was literally solved by the trail of blood. This led from the body in Victoria Road all the way back to the ship where there had been an altercation over the sexual favours of the captain's wife!

For a more genteel reminder of the town's history, however, a visit to 'A la Ronde' is recommended. This unique round house with an ornately decorated shell interior dates from 1795 when two much travelled spinster cousins decided to settle at Exmouth. They had the house built for them on land purchased by one of the cousins, Miss Jane Parminter, and it is said to be modelled on the circular style of San Vitale Church in Ravenna which they had previously visited on their European travels. The building is now in the care of the National Trust. Only a short distance away must be one of the smallest churches in the Country, Point in View. This, too, was built by the Parminters in 1811 together with almshouses. There is debate over whether the unusual name relates to the excellent views from here over the Exe Estuary or Miss Parminter's own religious point of view which apparently she pursued with vigour ... the conversion of Jews to Christianity!

Woodbury Common
Adders & Arson?

Just North of Exmouth, about three miles from the town centre, lies Woodbury Common, a vast expanse of open heath with its gorse and heather broken only by dotted clumps of Douglas firs and other pine trees. Part is still used for military training but there is much left for public recreation and it is a popular spot for walkers. The former strategic importance of this high ground is illustrated by Woodbury Castle, a large prehistoric hill fort, now neatly sliced in two by the main road. Nevertheless its deep defensive ditches still remain a popular playground for children.

Idyllic it may seem on a bright sunny day, with views over the Estuary or across to Budleigh Salterton and the sea beyond, but the Common is not without its dangers and darker secrets. The main danger is a natural one. Its bracken and short grass vegetation on the dry stony subsoil make it a popular home for the common viper or adder. Having said that, however, the chances of the ordinary rambler being bitten are extremely rare with odds of about one case every twenty years. Even then, the bite is seldom fatal for healthy adults.

As to its darker secrets, perhaps an event which happened in the late nineteen-eighties provides one example. It certainly gave a scare to one unwary rambler at the time. The chance discovery of a burnt-out car was the first of a bizarre set of events. Close examination of the wreckage revealed the burnt remains of a human corpse. As one can imagine, this led to a full-scale on-site investigation but searching police officers were not prepared for what they found. Close by there was a second burnt-out car and in it … another charred body! Gangland killing? Drugs-related murders? Mafia assassinations? Speculation was rife. For the crime reporters the solution was an anti-climax. Exhaustive enquiries revealed that there was no link between the two deaths. Both drivers had personal problems and sought a final solution. Unbeknown to each other they chose the same means and the same spot. It was a bizarre coincidence.

Such an occurrence would have been unheard of in the days of one of the area's most famous sons, Sir Walter Raleigh. It was on the fringe of the Common, towards East Budleigh, where he was born in 1552. The house, Hayes Barton, was built of cob around 1450 and is still very much in use today as a farm.

Budleigh Salterton
Millais and Murder

Dropping from the Common, past Hayes Barton, the coast is reached at Budleigh Salterton. It was here, at the end of the Promenade, that Sir John Millais painted his famous picture, 'The Boyhood of Raleigh'. The house where the artist stayed is opposite the site and identified by a plaque on the wall. Close by is the old police station where the back gate led onto the beach. The corpulent sergeant who was stationed there in the forties and fifties used to cross the pebble beach for a morning swim every day of the year. The replacement police station is situated further up the main street in a modern house.

Budleigh Salterton, sometimes locally referred to as just Salterton, derives its name from the salt pans which used to occupy the estuary of the River Otter but which today form a sanctuary for a host of seabirds. This area has a traditional link with smuggling as indeed has much of the East Devon coast. Such activities would have been much out of keeping with today's inhabitants. They have been the butt of many a music hall joke for Salterton is reputed to have more retired generals, admirals and judges living there than any other comparable town in the country.

However the peace of this small town was shattered when, in 1981, Juliet Rowe, the wife of a local millionaire business man, was shot dead at their home near the town's popular golf course. The weapon used was a .22 calibre, a size not generally associated with this type of crime. The fact that the alarms were not activated gave rise to all sorts of speculation, including the suggestion it could have been a professional 'hit'. Police enquiries ranged far and wide, even as far as Australia, but no solution was forthcoming. All the leads drew a blank and eventually the trail went cold although as in all murder cases the file was never closed. Some years later, towards the end of the decade, a kidnapping case in the Home Counties provided a break. The bizarre twist which brought the murderer to justice had its ending on the Haldon Hills and will be covered in the final chapter.

East Budleigh
The Smuggling Vicar

Only a short distance from Budleigh Salterton lies the small village of East Budleigh. In mediaeval days it had direct links to the sea via the River Otter. The village church would have been known to the young Walter Raleigh for his father was a churchwarden here. There are also links to Sir Francis Drake for he was Raleigh's cousin. More recent memorials in the church, however, relate to the Rev. Ambrose Stapleton and his family. One of the parish's longest-serving incumbents, he was the vicar here for some fifty-eight years, from 1794 to 1852. By all accounts he was a popular man who not only preached a good sermon but was noted for the aid he gave to the poor. But it was not for these saintly deeds he is best remembered but for his involvement in the smuggling trade, it being reputed that his vicarage was used as a store for barrels of contraband brandy.

Otterton
The 'French Connection'

Taking the back road to Sidmouth, via the very steep Peak Hill, the visitor will pass through East Budleigh's close neighbour, the village of Otterton with its 'French Connection'. No, not a connection with the drugs trade portrayed in the popular film of that title, but a religious one. Before the River Otter silted up, Otterton was a thriving port under the jurisdiction of the Benedictine Order from Mont St. Michael in Normandy and it was here, in the twelfth century, that they built their church. The chamber under the existing church is part of the foundations of that early building.

From the top of Peak Hill there are excellent views of the coast embracing the whole of Lyme Bay whilst below you see what can best be described as a pilot's view of Sidmouth. From the car park at the top of the hill popular trails extend northwards across Mutter's Moor, an expanse of gorse and heather not unlike Woodbury Common.

———————————— **Sidmouth** ————————————

International Folk Music and the Sainsbury Case

Sidmouth itself is normally a quiet town except for a couple of weeks each summer when it literally swings to the sound of music. The annual Sidmouth Folk Festival has earned an international reputation and attracts groups of performers from all over the world ... from the Alps to the Andes! Today's somewhat serene appearance has been deceptive on more than one occasion, however, as a report published in the *Exeter & Plymouth Gazette* on the 5th January, 1872, will show. This quotes from the Chief Constable's report to the Quarter Sessions wherein he stated that only through energetic action taken by the magistrates, local police officers and special constables sworn in for the occasion were serious disturbances averted during the previous Guy Fawkes night.

Recently the centre of Sidmouth has been tastefully restored with Victorian-style lampposts and semi-pedestrianisation thereby recapturing, to some extent, the atmosphere of what it may have been like when Queen Victoria visited the town in 1819 at the tender age of seven months.

Apart from the ubiquitous traffic, policing Sidmouth today has seldom given rise to the problems experienced in some other resorts. This made it even more sensational when the Sainsbury case hit the headlines in the summer of 1991 ... and we are not talking supermarket development in the town. Paul Sainsbury was a well-known local builder who had been reported missing in the autumn of the previous year after he had walked out on his common-law wife. Family and friends thought he had moved to the north of England to make a fresh start and nothing was heard of him for several months. It was only when his estranged common-law wife, bowed down by guilt, confessed her gruesome secret to a friend that the truth emerged. Paul Sainsbury was dead. More to the point she had strangled him with a nylon rope whilst he was asleep and, dismembering his body, had placed the pieces in a number of neatly-sealed plastic bags which were then thrown into a field. I had a graphic account of their discovery from one of the police officers engaged in the search who subsequently found the legs behind a hedge adjoining the A3052 road on the outskirts of Sidford. Other parts of the body lay nearby. In a later court hearing a story of physical abuse was unfolded and a plea of guilty to manslaughter on the grounds of diminished responsibility was accepted by the Judge. The accused walked free having been placed on probation for two years. She rejoined her two young children and has since moved away from the town. Without moralising on this particular case it does make one think ... what really is in those plastic bags one so often sees littering our roadside verges?

Salcombe Regis
The Body Snatchers

One grisly tale very often leads to another and the next story happened not so very far away. High on the other side of Sidmouth, above the River Sid, lies the small village of Salcombe Regis. I mention this only because of a reputed historical link to a particularly unsavoury crime of bygone years ... body snatching! Apparently the retaining bolt of the church's lych-gate is said to have been made from the shaft of an implement referred to as a 'resurrection corkscrew'. I have been unable to find this definition in the dictionary but it seems it was an important tool of the trade for body-snatchers. The particular tool from which the bolt is said to have been made was abandoned in the churchyard sometime around 1880 when two Sidmouth doctors, and their hired help, were surprised during the course of their gruesome work and fled from the scene. It is fair to say that the small booklet produced on the history of the church bears no reference to this incident although, on the other hand, it may be a matter they do not wish to publicise!

To the East of Salcome Regis, and lying on the shore at the end of a deep combe, is Weston Mouth. Approach is steep and difficult and little remains here except for a few small shacks.

However, in an earlier century, one of the beachside cottages was occupied by a member of the coastguard. His main task was to watch for smugglers whose lucrative trade was rife along this stretch of the coast.

——— Branscombe & Beer ———
Smuggling Country and Woe Betide the Exciseman

A couple of miles further east along the coast lies Branscombe. The church here predominantly dates from circa 1130 A.D., whilst the village itself formed part of the lands once owned by Alfred the Great. But the church is of special interest as it bears witness to some of our earlier social history. For instance, inside the church itself one will find a rare example of an early priest's room, a relic from the days when the priest lived alone and never moved far from his church. Then, with today's social trend towards the '2.4 kids' norm for families, pay a visit to the church's north transept and in particular to the conspicuous tomb which has been described as being like the front of a Greek temple. This marks the resting place of one Joan Tregarthen, a member of royal Plantagenet stock who died in 1583 having outlived two husbands and giving birth to some twenty children. But perhaps a more poignant reminder of the lawless days gone by will be found in the churchyard where, in the extreme south east corner is the raised tomb of John Hurley, aged 45, Custom House Officer of the parish, who died in August 1755. The full inscription has now become difficult to read but it bears witness to the fact that he fell to his death whilst investigating a signal fire lit by smugglers on top of the nearby cliffs. The truth is more likely to be that he was pushed over the cliffs to his death by the smugglers he went to arrest but no-one was ever brought to justice.

The coastal villages were close knit communities and none more so than neighbouring Beer. Smuggling, whilst romanticised in novels such as Daphne Du Maurier's *Jamaica Inn,* was nevertheless a cut-throat business and Beer was a thriving centre for this infamous trade. Its early reputation was such that no customs officer dared set foot there and the death of John Hurley bears witness to the depths to which some locals would stoop to safeguard their illegal pursuits.

But Beer's history has not always been so turbulent. There is evidence that the Romans quarried stone here and this unique product has been found in many early examples of their walls. Today these early quarries, and caves, are tourist attractions. A much gentler reminder of the past lies in its links with the lace trade which started when, in the late sixteenth century, Flemish immigrants brought their skills to East Devon. Although Honiton lace still enjoys an international reputation, few realise that at the height of the trade there were no fewer than four hundred registered lace makers in Beer and that part of Queen Victoria's wedding dress was made here.

But it was the sea to which Beer always turned in the end. Despite not having a harbour, only a beach-based fishing fleet, during the period between the wars it was the third largest port in Devon, when assessed in terms of tonnage and value of the catches. It is recorded that in December 1936 over half a million herrings were sold from the beach, a catch never surpassed, for sadly since then the large shoals have disappeared to find other feeding grounds.

Policing East Devon away from the coast has been equally as interesting and every village bobby would have had his share of stories to tell. But the tasks of the early law-enforcers were not always as we would understand them today.

Loughwood
The Chapel Hidden from the Law

Lying just north of the A35, between Honiton and Axminster, is Loughwood Farm with its early chapel. Now in the care of the National Trust, this small meeting house was built around 1653 to serve the Baptists of nearby Kilmington. The small thatched roof and cob wall building was, at that time, hidden in dense woods for its worshippers were a persecuted minority and the woodland cover enabled the preacher to hide from the Constabulary whose task it was to enforce the Act of Conformity. If he was lucky he ultimately made his escape across the nearby county boundary! The chapel is still furnished with box pews and an octagonal pulpit. Near the pulpit the floorboards can be lifted to reveal a hidden font large enough for adult baptism by total immersion, the waters being fed from a nearby spring.

Yarcombe
The Constabulary's Last Outpost

Some miles north of Loughwood, where the River Yarty flows under the A30 road and forms the county boundary between Devon and Somerset, lies the small village of Yarcombe. It has a long history which belies its minute size. The church, dominated by a fourteenth century tower, is the same age as the inn which was originally built as living quarters for the monks of Otterton Priory who were responsible for the administration of both the church and the manor. Two hundred years later the manor of Yarcombe was to pass into the hands of Sir Francis Drake. Still later, the inn was to serve as an important staging post for stagecoach passengers, changing its name from the 'Angel' to the 'Yarcombe Inn'. In recent times, however, the village has declined in importance. The village school closed in 1965 only to later reopen as a hotel and soon afterwards the village police station, which was the first of a row of houses going up the hill, suffered a similar fate when it passed into private ownership. The last outpost of the former Devon Constabulary was no more.

Dunkeswell
The Magna Carta and Kennedy Connections

North of the main London road lies the village of Dunkeswell. The historic interest here is more fundamentally linked to our basic freedoms than many would realise, the reason lying in the ruins of Dunkeswell Abbey. Of the abbey, which was founded for the Cistercian Order in 1201, very little survives apart from a few walls and a ruined gate-house. It is believed, however, that within the ruins lied the remains of its founder, William Brewer. Although I have not seen the document I understand that he, with King John, was one of the signatories of the Magna Carta.

Today, the main interests are centred on the airfield and nearby Wolford Chapel, both having trans-Atlantic connections. The airfield is only a shadow of its former self but is nevertheless home to both flying and parachute clubs. Its annual air day has often produced aircraft from the nostalgic past, including some from the United States. This is not surprising because during the war it was home to the 7th U.S. Navy Air Wing, operating Liberator and Catalina aircraft. It was whilst based here that, Joseph, the eldest brother of J. F. Kennedy, former President of the United States, lost his life. He, and others, are commemorated in the Parish Church where there is a book of remembrance. Wolford Chapel's link is with Canada. Wolford was once the home of John Graves Simcoe, the first Lt. Governor of the Province of Upper Canada. In 1966 the Chapel and its surrounding land was given to the Canadian Province of Ontario and is now deemed to be Canadian territory. Signposts to the Chapel display the maple leaf emblem.

Culmstock & Clayhidon
The Drunken Woman and the Murdered Surveyor

About four miles from Dunkeswell, by minor roads, lies the village of Culmstock. I refer to it only because of a report taken from a 1902 edition of the *Devon Weekly Times,* and subsequently reproduced in *Out of the Blue — a History of the Devon Constabulary,* which illustrates only too well the important role that policemen's wives were expected to play in rural communities. The press report refers to a case concerning one Ellen Snow, a respectably-dressed middle-aged woman, who pleaded not guilty to being drunk on the highway at Culmstock on March 7th 1902. It appears that the local policeman, a P.C. Popham, was away on duty in connection with a royal visit so his wife was called to the scene. She found the woman had two bottles of gin, each half empty, and said in her opinion there was no doubt the woman was drunk. The magistrates convicted and fined the accused ten shillings. If, however, you visit the village make a point of looking at the top of the tower on the parish church. You should see a yew tree which is reputed to have been growing there for over 250 years. Also a mile north is Culmstock Beacon, over 850 feet above sea level. If you make the climb to the top look out for a 'beehive' hut thought to be a beacon of pre-Elizabethan origin.

But crime in Devon's rural villages was not limited to drunkenness. A mere four miles from Culmstock lies another small village, Clayhidon. Here, close to where a bridge crosses the young River Culm, a plaque bears witness to evil deeds with the legend, "William Blackmore, Land Surveyor of Clayhidon Mills, was murdered on this spot, the 6th day of February, 1853 by George Sparks of this parish who was executed at Exeter for his horrid crime."

Honiton

The Salvation Army Riots

Leaving the leafy lanes behind we now return towards Exeter with a detour off the main road into the town of Honiton, now thankfully freed from serious traffic problems as a result of its by-pass. The wide main High Street owes its breadth to some extent to the two great fires which ravaged the town in the eighteenth century. This was the main stage route to London and, as such, featured a number of coaching inns, many of which still stand today. The extra width also allows a weekly street market to be held with some of the stalls backing onto a conduit, now mostly covered. This was where, in the years before piped water, the locals used to draw their drinking supply. But as today's peaceful High Street shoppers pass the church, with its hundred foot high tower, I wonder how many realise the extent to which religious intolerance used to exist in the town.

The poor victims of the townfolks' wrath was none other than the Salvation Army, then in its evangelical infancy. A graphic report in the *Devon Weekly Times,* dated 22nd December 1882, records how a serious disturbance occurred when the Salvation Army members met protesters in the High Street. Stones, flour and other items were hurled and considerable injuries caused, one Army member almost losing an eye. Extra policemen had been called in anticipation of unrest but they were no match for the estimated crowd of two thousand that took to the streets. There was also a report of a pistol being discharged during the disturbance.

The Salvationists were not the only army to be based in Honiton which for years was a military base for the R.E.M.E. Changing logistic requirements, however, saw the closure of Heathfield Camp in the nineteen-sixties but there was one final use for the buildings before they were demolished to make way for a modern housing estate. For many Asian Ugandans Honiton was their first taste of the west after they fled from the persecutions of the dictator, Idi Amin. For a while, until assimilated into the wider community, Heathfield Camp was their home.

Ottery St Mary
Tar Barrels and Blunderbusses

In the context of today's policing of East Devon perhaps the single event which calls most for increased resources on the day must be the annual carnival at Ottery St. Mary. This is normally held on Guy Fawkes Day, and it is not only the local Constabulary which has cause to be wary but the County's Fire Service as well. Following a tradition which started in the eighteenth century, today's revellers run through the crowded main street carrying blazing tar barrels, frequently handing them on from one to another. But police supervision was not always appreciated as a report of April 1859 makes clear following a complaint that the police had interfered too much. In defence of the Force it was pointed out that the Inspector's excessive zeal was partly due to the fact that, as well as the tar barrels, guns and blunderbusses were being discharged in the street! Fortunately such events are unheard of today and fires and injuries are surprisingly rare. One of the last really big fires in the town started in Yonder Street, no on Guy Fawkes Day, but on a hot summer's day in 1866. On that occasion the flames are reported to have swept though all the thatched houses from one end of the town to another and the resulting devastation was apparently recorded in the *London Illustrated News*.

The old police station used to stand at the top of the hill opposite the fine church, but today it is no longer used as such. Policing trends have decreed that a solitary community policeman replaces the former sectional status which had a number of police officers under the supervision of a Sergeant.

One example of policing Ottery St. Mary in earlier days, and of the discipline code, will be found in Force Orders dated 25th February 1868. Here the entry refers to 3rd Class Constable No. 78 who was stationed in the town. The officer had been found guilty of gross misconduct in that he went into a public house on a Sunday, during prohibited hours, and demanded a beer. He apparently told the landlord that he had a right to demand a beer at any hour on a Sunday provided he paid for it! He was fined ten shillings, which was half a week's pay in those days, and severely reprimanded with a warning that if there was any repetition of such conduct he would be brought before the magistrates with a recommendation he be sent to prison.

However, it is to the church we must look for much of the

town's history for this is an institution which seemingly never changes. The church of St. Mary is remarkable in that it is said to have been built to resemble Exeter Cathedral and is therefore out of all proportion to the size one would normally expect to find in a small town. Its resemblance to the cathedral is not surprising, however, when one realises that it was rebuilt around 1335 by Bishop Grandisson, who was the Bishop of Exeter, and who founded a college for forty monks on this site. The tomb of Sir Otho de Grandisson, who died in 1359, lies within the church.

Whimple
The Murder of P.C. Potter

Returning towards Exeter along the main A30 road you will note the signpost pointing to Whimple, a small village lying a mile off the main road to your right. Until a few years ago Whimple was arguably the most famous producer of cider in Britain. Advertisements proclaiming 'Whiteways of Whimple' could be seen everywhere and its large fermenting and bottling plants were set amidst some of the country's finest orchards. Sadly new E.U. regulations from Brussels compounded with other problems has seen the plant fall slowly into disuse. It was whilst it was in its heyday, however, that it was the scene of one of the most horrific crimes to hit the former Devon Constabulary.

P.C. Potter was the local policeman who, suspecting pilfering from Whiteways' premises, set up observations within their offices. During the evening of 17th January, 1938, whilst keeping watch, he surprised two young men from the village as they broke into the office where he was hiding. One immediately made good his escape but the other viciously attacked the officer and left him bleeding before he, too, made his exit. When P.C. Potter failed to return home at the end of his late shift his wife telephoned his superiors who were not too perturbed at first. It was not unusual for policemen to work late. However, as the hours passed so fears grew and a search was finally implemented. It was the Managing Director of the factory, Mr Ronald Whiteway, who on arriving for work at 7 a.m. discovered the policeman lying bleeding, in his office and unable to move. P.C. Potter was rushed to hospital and local enquiries soon traced the culprits through fingerprints found at the scene. They were charged with burglary and causing grievous bodily harm with intent to murder.

Unfortunately for all concerned, however, P.C. Potter's injuries were to prove fatal and sixteen days later, on the 2nd February, he passed away. The charge against the two men was changed to murder.

At the subsequent trial the jury accepted the plea of one of the men, Leslie Downing, that he had left the scene before the assault took place. He was sentenced to twelve months for imprisonment. The other man, Stanley Martin, was sentenced to death for murder. This was subsequently commuted to life imprisonment.

To pause in the attractive village square in front of the church one can hardly imagine a foul murder happening in such a peaceful spot and yet it serves to illustrate that police officers can at any time, or place, meet circumstances which may cost them their lives.

———— Aylesbeare ————
The Genette Tate Mystery

This first chapter, on East Devon, would not be complete without some mention of an unsolved mystery which has taxed the local Force ever since August 1978. I refer to Genette Tate and a story which held the headlines of the nations' press for many weeks. Genette, a thirteen-year-old schoolgirl, lived in the village of Aylesbeare, not far from the main runway of Exeter Airport. On the fateful day she set out on what, for her, was a normal routine ... delivering the evening papers on her bicycle. Her route took her down one of the country lanes where she paused to speak to a couple of her school chums before cycling ahead to make another delivery. Only minutes later her friends came across the cycle lying on its side in the lane with the rear wheel still spinning. Of Genette there was no trace. In fact she has never been seen again. In a lane barely wide enough to take traffic, her friends were adamant they had seen nothing untoward. There had been no other traffic, neither had they seen any other persons. A huge search was undertaken and at one stage over seven thousand people turned out to minutely probe nearby Woodbury Common. Thermal-imaging cameras were used from the air whilst frogmen searched every pond and stream in the area, making over four hundred dives. Mounted police officers from other forces and searcher dogs all joined in the search but to no avail. Suspicion fell on certain characters but enquiries always drew a blank. Fear stalked the village. The fact that Genette disappeared so quickly, and without any trace whatsoever, brought those with experience of the paranormal flocking to Aylesbeare. But even the mystics could throw no tangible light on the mystery. Abduction by extra-terrestrials seemed as likely a solution as many others that were expounded at the time. Even today, Genette is not forgotten and her file remains open at police headquarters. Every time reports are received of unidentified bodies of young girls being found contact is made with the Force concerned. The horrific case of the serial killings at 25 Cromwell Place, Gloucester, in 1994, is a prime example of when Genette's file comes to the fore yet again. For her family and the villagers the nightmare still lingers and probably will as long as the mystery remains unsolved.

*Chambercombe Manor, where the skeleton of a woman
was discovered within a sealed room*

Chapter 2
North Devon

Bideford

The Three Witches and the Buried Parson

The Autumn of 1953 was to see the first of my two spells of duty in North Devon when I arrived at Bideford, a town associated with the writings of Charles Kingsley and *Westward Ho!* in particular. Divided by the River Torridge, the two halves of the town are linked by a bridge of mediaeval origin which has no less than two dozen arches, each of different size. This irregularity has been explained by the fact that the original was timber-built and the length of the spans corresponded with that of the wood available at the time. When it was subsequently strengthened by stone in the mid-fifteenth century, the builders merely placed the new materials around the existing wooden structure. However, another explanation is that each arch was financed by local merchants and therefore varied according to their wealth. I suppose one story is as good as the other!

Standing high on a ramp on the west bank of the river about a hundred yards from the bridge is Bideford Police Station. It is a large red brick building which was built in 1898, a date which virtually coincided with the small, but independent, Bideford Borough Police Force joining the Devon Constabulary. At that time the force comprised only three men. Its Head Constable accepted a position as Sergeant in the larger force and the pay of the two Constables was increased by 1/2d per week. The only other significant changes to the building over the years are that married quarters, which used to flank the large red-tiled entrance hall, have been turned into additional office space.

The town, whilst very pleasant, has few sites of special historic interest to offer today's visitors. It is hard to realise that in the Elizabethan era it was one of the busiest ports in the country or that between 1700 and 1755 most of Britain's tobacco was imported through here. The Quay is still used for shipping although the size of vessels is somewhat restricted by the silting up of the Torridge. Nevertheless there are few ports, small or otherwise, where cargo ships moor in the centre of town alongside one of the main shopping streets.

With its prominence as a port during the 16th century perhaps it is no surprise that the town's most famous son was one of the Elizabethan era's greatest seafarers, Sir Richard Grenville. He was particularly noted for his exploits during the Spanish Armada, and later, when off the Azores, his small ship the *Revenge,* engaged single-handedly a fleet of fifteen Spanish men-of-war.

Another noted local nobleman, but for completely different reasons, was Sir William Coffin. His was an appropriate name as it turned out. He was a prominent courtier and owned estates in the area but it seems that his moment in history came during the period between 1514 and 1524 when the vicar of the parish church of St. Mary was the Rev. Richard Gilbert. It appears that Sir William was passing the churchyard one day when he noticed a disturbance. On investigating he discovered that the family of a poor peasant farmer were arguing with the vicar who was refusing to bury the deceased unless the family paid in advance by giving him the farmer's only legacy ... a cow. Sir William immediately stepped into the row and told the Rev. Gilbert that if he did not bury the farmer he would see he was buried instead. The vicar refused whereupon he was thrown into the empty grave and the onlookers needed no bidding in helping to shovel earth upon the now terrified priest. As his head was about to disappear the vicar relented, was released and carried on with the service. That was not the end of the matter, however, because later the vicar complained. Assaulting a priest was a capital offence in those days and Sir William was arraigned before Parliament for trial by his peers. Fortunately he was an eloquent speaker and had friends in the House who sympathised with his views. The far-reaching outcome was that instead of Sir William being punished, as a man of lesser standing undoubtedly would have been, Parliament laid down a Mortuary Act which established rules for burials and the costs which could be levied. Today, apart from the bridge, remains of an historic past are difficult to find. One exception is Chudleigh Fort which was built by Maj. Gen. Chudleigh for the parliamentary forces in 1642. This defensive site, with some of its cannons, overlooks the river from a hillside park at East-the-Water.

My most vivid recollection of duty in the town is a chilling one and yet it does not involve any crime. It was indeed a cold November night and I was scheduled to make a 'point' at the telephone kiosk situated near the Handy Cross Cemetery on the outskirts of town. In the days before personal radios 'points' were made every hour at various locations where an officer could be reached by telephone if required. On this particular night my 'point' was at 1.30 a.m. and I was due to finish at 2 a.m. The timing was one example of how the system ensured you gave a full eight hours of duty. The 'point' lasted ten minutes so it would be at least 1.40 a.m. before you left for the police station and the end of the shift ... and that was two miles away!

No only was it a cold night but there was a full moon. A strong wind blew whispy clouds across the moon's face causing moving shadows on the ground whilst at the same time its flow caused the telegraph wires to hum.

An owl hooted from somewhere on the far side of the churchyard. Ten minutes seemed an eternity and the imagination played tricks. The sudden clanking of chains from the cemetery was not imagination however and in an instant I discovered why policemen wore helmets. It was to provide space for hair to stand on end!

So what was it? I didn't stop long enough to discover the cause that night. But in the rational light of day I came to the conclusion there must have been a logical explanation. And there was. I learnt that in the cemetery was a small pump-house and that probably what I had heard was the pump coming into operation. The clink of chains had been the clunk of machinery ... or was it?!

I would add that this incident occurred before I heard the story of the three witches who used to live, I believe, in Higher

Gunstone Lane. Significantly, their old thatched cottage was burnt to the ground over a century ago. They faced trial in 1682 following charges brought by some of the town's more susceptible inhabitants. Evidence of wax images and the use of pins was given to substantiate the charges. It is likely the accused were just three old 'hags' but their conduct during interrogation didn't help them and they were found guilty. Sentence was carried out on the 25th August, 1682, at the Heavitree Gallows, Exeter. Reports describe how the three of them were left to hang in a row, the last to die being Temperance Lloyd. However, she did not have the distinction of being the last person to be hanged for witchcraft at Exeter. That record went two years later, in 1684, to an Alice Molland. Today, thousands of motorists in Exeter drive past the site of those gallows each week without realising that they used to stand on the main London road (A30), near the junction of Heavitree Road with Sidmouth Road. The site is now occupied by a filling station which, until twenty years ago, was always known as 'The Gallows'.

Bideford was a close-knit town and like most of North Devon had suffered isolation from the rest of the County through lack of a good communications system. Fortunately this has recently been redressed to some extent by the new North Devon Link Road although this has its critics who say it is still inadequate.

The town appeared to be a centre of lawlessness at the turn of the century and a report to the standing joint committee held in February 1899 highlighted a number of problems faced by the local police. In one incident it was reported that they were "mobbed, kicked and knocked about". But from these contemporary reports it also appeared that making complaints against the police is far from being a recent trend. Unfortunately for Bideford's police some of the more unruly elements in the town were making a good living out of it, collecting monies for their defence and pocketing the surplus. Whereupon they would get arrested again, make yet another complaint and start further collections from the townsfolk. It was also said that the Justices gave the police little backing by giving such derisory fines that it paid the law-breakers to re-offend.

Appledore

The Launching of the Pacific Sandpiper

A couple of miles downstream from Bideford lies Appledore at the mouth of the Taw and Torridge estuaries. I heard many tales of how it always took two policemen to patrol the quay in the days of the sailing ships. And these were always hand-picked for their brawn rather than brain! No doubt it would have been equally hazardous policing the maze of narrow streets which still lies behind the river frontage and where Elizabethan houses mingle with the later Georgian architecture. In fact it is a pleasant experience to read their names as you pass by. See if you can find 'Hove to', 'Cockle Cottage', 'Lantern Cottage' or 'Gulls' Cry' to name but a few of them.

Shipbuilding has always been a feature of Appledore and its history locally can be traced back at least as far as the reign of Elizabeth the First. It is still carried on today and enjoys a fine reputation. When the present facilities were built they contained the largest covered dry dock in Europe.

It was to be this industry which briefly brought me back to North Devon in the mid nineteen-eighties. Appledore Shipbuilders had just completed building the *Pacific Sandpiper,* a cargo vessel with an overall length of some 104 metres and a dead-weight of approximately 3,200 tonnes. But it was a cargo vessel with a difference. It was built for Pacific Nuclear Transport Plc and was a nuclear fuels carrier destined to carry nuclear waste between Japan and the U.K. As one can imagine, the launching not only brought a number of dignitaries to the ceremony but attracted a core of nuclear protesters as well. The local police in keeping order were alleged to have made a number of 'illegal' arrests and an investigation was ordered under the auspices of the statutory Police Complaints Authority. As an independent senior officer I was deputed to act as their Investigating Officer ... and thus returned to a small town which, for me, epitomises the best of the seafaring traditions of the North Devon coast.

But perhaps an epitaph on a headstone in the parish churchyard portrays the simple philosophy of local seafarers best of all. It reads:

Life's stormy voyage is ended, over the bar at last,
With Jesus as trusted pilot, peril and danger past;
Safe anchored in the harbour, safe on heavenly shore,
No log book tells my story, I feel safe for evermore.

Barnstaple

At Home in the Prison

My second spell in North Devon came in 1960 when I was posted to the Divisional Police Headquarters at Barnstaple as a member of the Force's Traffic department. The 'beat' was a wide ranging one, from the Cornish boundary in the west to the County line with Somerset in the east. We travelled south to Lapford and also as far as Holsworthy and Hatherleigh. Much of Exmoor, too, came within our patrol area.

Barnstaple is North Devon's principal town and reputed to be the country's oldest borough. By tradition it traces its charter back to the reign of Athlestan and the year 830 A.D. Certainly there was a Norman stronghold here and the mound still remains close to the town's market. Elsewhere in the town are little gems to remind one of its past history. For instance, St Anne's Chapel is situated in pleasant grounds between the two main thoroughfares, High Street and Boutport Street, and under the twisted spire of the parish church. The chapel dates from the fourteenth Century but from the mid-sixteenth Century until 1908 served as a Grammar School. One of its more famous pupils was John Gay, the author of 'The Beggars' Opera.' Today it is a museum and still contains the trappings of those early school days. Close by, in a little cobbled alley, are almshouses dating back almost three and a half centuries. Near the Quay, and the present day bus station, is Queen Anne's Walk. Built around 1700 in classical style it used to be a meeting place for merchants and shipowners in the days before the River Taw silted up and Barnstaple lost its importance as a port. Between the columns is the 'Tome Stone' which was originally erected in 1633 and across which the merchants would strike their deals.

Further along from Queen Anne's Walk lies the former Barnstaple Town Railway Station. Since closing it has had a number of uses, including that of a restaurant, whilst the signal box has been turned into a small museum with relics from the former Barnstaple & Lynmouth Railway. But it is to a site almost opposite the former station that my memories take me. Unfortunately the buildings themselves no longer exist.

The site was next to the old police station which was built in 1926 and now serves as offices for the Probation Service. From the road those passing by would only see two red-brick houses with arched windows, high pointed gables and very decorative brickwork so much loved by the Victorians. They were separated by an ornate semi-castellated arch from which hung large, solid, wooden gates. At the time of my stay in Barnstaple they were used as married quarters for two police officers.

What could not be seen from the road, however, were the small stable, wash-house and a few remains of the nineteenth century prison which lay behind. This was built in 1874, at a cost of £3172, had 32 cells and an exercise yard. Records show that in 1875 it housed a total of 76 prisoners with a maximum of 19 at any one time. Total running costs in that year amounted to £359.2s.0d. In 1878, as a result of the Prisons Act which made it mandatory for all prisoners to go to the County Gaol in Exeter, it was officially closed. It then adopted a secondary use as an isolation hospital, with a decontamination room, but even this function ceased in 1932 when the premises were used as a warehouse and the yard was opened up as part of the cattle market. By the time we arrived in 1960 most of the prison, other than the two houses, had been cleared, the whole site finally being demolished in 1978.

The house to the right of the entrance gates were, we had been told, once used by the prison's governor and the other by the warder. I was able to confirm this and found an entry in the *County Directory* for 1878 to the effect that the Governor was a Richard Webber and his wife acted as the matron. Needless to say when my wife and I moved to Barnstaple, we felt 'privileged' to be occupying the former 'governor's' house. But it was far from luxury. Built before the days of damp courses, every time spring tides made the river levels rise above normal the effects were felt in our home only a street's width away from the Quay. Even today, the new car park on the Quay carries a warning of flooding at high tides! The larder which lay down a passage off the kitchen was the size of some modern lounges and the high ceiling was festooned with hooks for hanging sides of meat ... or the prisoners! And off the room we used as a lounge was another small ante-room where the temperature was always chilly ... even in mid-summer. But the most spooky of all was the feeling that we were not alone. In fact we are convinced that a poltergeist was present although fortunately for us it was only mildly mischievous and not malevolent. The principle manifestation was that things moved although we never actually saw it happen. Objects we knew to be in a certain place would disappear only to be found later where we had not been. Visitors also remarked on the building's 'atmosphere'. But for us it was not an unhappy house. Our eldest son was born whilst we were there.

It is perhaps of interest for the reader to record a few early facts about policing the Borough. In the first half of the nineteenth century Barnstaple was policed by three part-timers who couldn't keep order. Things became so bad that in 1840, after a spate of burglaries, the Mayor wrote to the Home Secretary and asked that an efficient police officer be sent to clear up the crime. This officer was to remain 'incognito' with only the Mayor and the Town Clerk knowing his identity.

In answer to the plea an officer called Charles Oatway was despatched from London. We do not know if he was successful because the only record of his visit was that he was "violently and grossly assaulted and beaten by three men near Barnstaple Bridge". It is further recorded that the attack cost the Council £7 in medical expenses and compensation which would have been the equivalent of almost two months' pay.

Following this 'fiasco' it was decided to engage an 'efficient Superintendent' and a David Steel of the Metropolitan Police was appointed at an annual salary of £100. His first report to the

Watch Committee expressed his concern at the high degree of drunkenness and prostitution in the town. Indicative of the state of the local police was that within a month of his arrival two of the Constables were themselves dismissed for drunkenness. However things slowly improved and between 1861 and 1900 the number of police officers rose from five to thirteen.

Records of punishment inflicted on prisoners in Barnstaple during those early lawless Victorian days included incarceration in a wooden cage, being flogged on the gate of the Corn Market or being flogged around town for which there was a set procedure. One of the Mayors of the day so liked this method of punishment that he earned the nickname of 'The Whipping Mayor.'

There is also a much earlier record that in 1590 the Spring Assizes were switched from Exeter to Barnstaple because of an outbreak of plague in the city. At the end of the hearing eighteen prisoners were hung on Castle Green, opposite today's modern police station.

Wreckers' Coast

But to return to more modern times and the traffic patrol beat which took us from Barnstaple to the Cornish Boundary. Hartland with its wild promontory jutting out into the Atlantic Ocean, fell within our area as did its lighthouse which flashed a constant warning to shipping using the Bristol Channel. Unfortunately its message all too frequently failed and the crews of the Clovelly and Appledore lifeboats were amongst the bravest and hardest working to be found anywhere. If their missions failed then it was local police officers who had the unenviable task of dealing with the sailors' bodies when they came ashore and attending the post-mortems which invariably followed. In fact I recall one winter's night during my days at Bideford when a coaster foundered. The following day we retrieved a number of bodies. An old local rhyme succinctly sums up the reputation of this stretch of coast. Quite simply it reads,

From Morteboe Point to Hartland Light,
A sailors' death both day and night.

Hartland

Jagged Rocks and Knarled Old Stocks

If visiting Hartland it is worth travelling the extra three miles to the Quay. Little is there except a few old cottages and a hotel, all exposed to the full force of westerly winds. The Quay, by which it is still known, was destroyed by storms a century ago. But pause and look at the rocks and cliff face behind. The jagged rocks pierce the water's surface like rows of shark's teeth and often the water here is white with rage. It takes little imagination to understand the fate which awaits any vessels which venture too near.

However, it was the story of a wicked vicar that brought me to the village. With ingredients of sex and murder it seemed like a good case to investigate even though an account of the Rev. Peter Vine had already been published elsewhere. But my investigation proved futile. Searches of church files, local and county records offices all drew a blank, so did by and large talking to the locals, including a member of the Vine family. A very pleasant hour with a retired vicar of the parish at first provided a ray of hope but this was quickly dashed. He was a local historian and author and had heard the story which naturally intrigued him. His own family had lived in the parish since the sixteenth century and the first he had heard of the alleged crimes of the Rev. Vine was only twenty years ago and yet the murder was supposed to have happened in 1811. He, too, had found no record that such an evil vicar had ever been at Hartland and so my trail for another story grew cold. Or did it? The mystery now is how did the legend of the evil vicar of Hartland start in the first place?

It was not altogether a wasted journey, however, for in the ancient church is a small room known as the Pope's Chamber where the priest or watchmen used to stand guard. Hidden behind a dark wooden door, it is reached by a short flight of stone steps. Now a small museum, its exhibits include the village stocks.

Many unusual events seem either to occur near churches or involve the clergy. Quite close to Hartland, but actually just over the boundary in Cornwall, another grisly event unfolded. But this happened less than twenty years ago and is well documented. A local undertaker informed the police that he had found a disturbed grave in the local cemetery. Following an exhumation it was discovered that parts of the body were missing, whilst in the grave were a candle and holder which had been stolen earlier from the church. Later a book on black magic was stolen from the local library. But the thief had left a footprint. Police enquiries led them to the home of a youth where they found footwear matching a library print. They were not so prepared for what they found next - a skull in his wardrobe!

Heatherleigh
Riverside Murder of Artist

One of the furthest points we visited during our traffic patrols from Barnstaple was the small town of Hatherleigh. Today's main events are the weekly market and the annual carnival, both of which are always well attended. In 1905, however, Heatherleigh was 'put on the map' for a tragic episode which sadly illustrates that deaths of persons held in custody are not a modern phenomenon.

The case to which I refer started with the death, in 1905, of one Mary Breton who was aged 33 and a regular visitor to Hatherleigh where she stayed with her uncle. By all accounts she was an accomplished artist and was frequently seen with her easel sketching and painting local landscapes. When, on the 15th May, she left to continue painting a riverside scene in the Strawbridge Pathfields she promised to be back for dinner. When she did not return fears arose and a search was quickly organised. Her easel and half finished painting were found near the river and nearby lay her body. Her head was covered in blood, having been battered almost to a point where she could not be recognised. It was noticed at the time that her skirt was wet. There was no sign of life.

The next stage shows only too well how far the investigation of crime has progressed during this century with the advancement of modern techniques and forensic science. In Mary Breton's case the local Coroner insisted on holding the inquest the following day. The only evidence available at that time was a description of her injuries and the location of the body, with the added information that there were cattle in the field. On this alone the Coroner deduced that, whilst sitting at her easel, she had been charged from behind by one of the herd, possibly a bullock, the horns of which had inflicted the injuries to her head. The jury then returned a verdict that Miss Breton had died from haemorrhage resulting from injuries to the head, there being no evidence to show their cause.

Fortunately the local police did not let the situation rest there. Rumours were becoming rife concerning a Jack Ware who had recently returned to Heatherleigh after an absence of several years. It quickly became known that he had recently been released from Exeter prison having served a twelve-month sentence for indecently assaulting another woman elsewhere in the County. By now the bullock theory was beginning to wear thin. Enquiries into Ware's movements were made by Sergeant Hill, who was the officer in charge of the local police contingent. He ascertained that on the night of the murder Ware had been drinking in the town's London Hotel where he appeared very agitated. Furthermore customers had noticed that his boots and trousers were wet and muddy. Then, on the day of the inquest, Ware failed to turn up for work. The following day he changed his place of employment and that is where Sergeant Hill caught up with him. He questioned Ware but the answers gave cause for doubt so the Sergeant told him he was taking him to Hatherleigh Police Station whilst they made further checks on his movements during the night of the murder.

Subsequent examination of the scene revealed blood-stained stones on the river bed and signs of a struggle. It was obvious that the deceased's injuries had been caused by the stones being used as an instrument and the bullock theory was immediately discounted. But the weight of this new evidence was never put to Ware.

About forty-five minutes after Ware had been placed in the cell at Hatherleigh Police Station, Constable Smith paid him a routine visit. He was not prepared, however, for the sight he saw as he looked through the hatch in the cell door. There, lying on the cell floor, was the body of John Ware. A scarf was tied tightly around his neck and blood was pouring from a head wound and from his ears. It appeared that he had stood on the hard wooden cell bed and knotted the scarf around his neck. As he lost consciousness he fell, striking his head on the floor. A doctor pronounced life extinct and certified cause of death as being due to strangulation. At the inquest the jury upheld this view and gave its verdict that death was self-inflicted whilst of sound mind and that he had killed himself out of fear of punishment. They also added a rider that the actions of detaining Ware were completely justified and that neither Constable Smith or any other officer, were to blame in any way for the death.

The murderer of Mary Breton was never brought to justice but fate, in its own way, had seen justice done.

Lapford
The Haunting Rector

Our patrol of the main A377 road, between Barnstaple and Exeter, ended at Lapford. The police house, no longer used as such, was on the main road, not far from the railway station. The main village lay up the hill about a mile away and it was there that another tale of folklore has been spawned.

The story is one which a member of the local Special Constabulary confirms still lies at the back of the mind of some of the village's older residents although events get more vague with the passage of time. At the same time a former Rector of the parish would not discuss it with me at all as he felt the story should not be perpetuated, a view which I suppose is not all that surprising seeing it concerned one of his predecessors. The events to which I refer occurred between 1825–1861 when the Rector at Lapford was one John Arundel Radford whose grave lies near the east end of the parish church. By all accounts he was possessed by a devil and had no concept of morality. It is alleged that his powers kept the villagers in a state of complete terror and no woman was safe from his advances. Furthermore he owed money far and wide and had amassed considerable debts. When the Bishop heard of this sorry state of affairs he sent a curate to observe the Rev. Radford and report back on his findings. Unfortunately the poor man was apparently found dead soon after his arrival. Like so often is the case with country folklore I have heard two versions. One says the curate had his throat cut. The other says he was found hanging from a beam in the rectory. What seems to be not in doubt is the fact that the Rector was charged with murder but, as there was no proof against him, he was subsequently acquitted and returned to his living at Lapford.

That is not the end of the story, however, and the local legend grew. In his will the Rev. Radford apparently asked that he be buried within the church, adding a rider that if his wishes were not followed the villagers would be cursed. In view of past events, the Church Council could not agree to the request and so the body was interred outside. Following the burial two phenomena are said to have occurred. One was that the cross marking the grave would not stand erect until finally it was concreted firmly into place. Secondly, a small hole appeared and no matter what steps were taken to seal the grave none were successful. Some villagers still say that the body does not rest at ease but rises through the hole at night to return to the site of the old rectory. We, on the other hand, return to Barnstaple and head towards the North Devon coast again.

--------------------- **Braunton** ---------------------
Burrows and Bows

This small town, just north of Barnstaple, is recognised internationally for the Burrows, a National Nature Reserve with one of the largest sand-dune systems in Britain, with some dunes reaching a height of almost one hundred feet. The Countryside Centre, near the main car park, contains displays of local flora and fauna. For a reminder of the past, however, why not visit 'The Butts'. This small path runs parallel to the stream near the churchyard but is now bisected by the main road at Butts Bridge. It was here, long ago, that the 'feudal' peasant army had to practice with their long bows after leaving church. Only a mile away, the Royal Air Force Station at Chivenor, with its modern jet aircraft, for years showed how far the nation's defences have advanced since then. Sadly, however, following a defence review the base was scheduled for closure at the end of 1994.

--------------------- **Georgeham** ---------------------
The Tarka Trail Connection

From Braunton take the scenic coast road to Ilfracombe where parking bays alongside the B3231 provide almost aerial views across the Burrows and Saunton Sands. I have heard that an ancient settlement lies buried there but, if there is, no signs are visible today. The road is narrow and by no means straight, passing through the villages of Croyde and Georgeham, on the way to Woolacombe. The best surfing beaches in the County will be found near here.

Those lovers of literature who have read and enjoyed Henry Williamson's classic tale *Tarka the Otter* may be interested to know that it was written, during the 1920s, whilst the author was living in a small cottage at Georgeham. Today, the journeys made by the legendary otter are traced by 'The Tarka Trail'. These 180 miles of footpath are part of a major countryside and environmental project officially opened by Prince Charles in May 1992 and lie almost wholly within North Devon.

Mortehoe
Death and Duckings

This small village lies just North of Woolacombe and close to Morte Point. Rocks just offshore make it particularly dangerous for inshore shipping and, as its name suggests, it has a fatal reputation. The small church here is frequently mentioned in guide books partly because of its age but mainly because of a connection to Sir William Tracey. He was one of the four knights who, following King Henry II's quarrel with his Chancellor and Archbishop, Thomas a Beckett, slew the Church's leader within his own Cathedral at Canterbury. The Tracey family had many estates in Devon, including Bovey Tracey, and it was believed he came to the isolation of Mortehoe to do penance after his unholy crime. In recent years, however, this theory has been disproved and the ancient tomb within the church is now considered to be that of a different William Tracey who was Rector of the Parish until his death in 1322. Sadly, the church is often locked. Nearby was the village duck-pool. Not for our feathered friends, however, but for ducking "fraudulent traders, scolds and unquiet women." Now drained, only the depression remains and that is on private land.

Ilfracombe
The Mysteries of the Skeleton and the Legless Corpse

The premier resort on Devon's north coast must be Ilfracombe, a generally quiet spot which seems to be in a time-warp compared with some of the south coast's livelier counterparts. The old Police Station, in the lower part of the town near the coach park, was built of red-brick in a style popular in the nineteen-twenties. The Sergeant's quarters formed part of the building being strategically placed between the police office and the public conveniences next door. Or, as one Sergeant succinctly put it, between the felons and the flushes. The premises were sold around 1970 and shortly after reopened as a night club under the appropriate name of 'La Bastille'. Its sign ... a guillotine!

One story told to me by a former resident of the Sergeant's house could have had unfortunate repercussions had it not been for his eagle eye. Whilst in the back yard one day he saw a rope, one end of which was tied to a drain pipe. The other end dangled over the wall ... into the yard used to exercise the prisoners. Recognising the rope he taxed his young children. "Yes daddy," they chorused, "It's there to help the prisoners escape!" Such a story goes to show, however, how closely policemen's families lived as part of 'the job' just a few short years ago.

The North Devon coast, on which Ilfracombe just about occupies central position, enjoyed a certain notoriety for smuggling exploits on a par with the south of the County. Wrecking along this stretch of the coast seems to have been a common pursuit. So too, to a lesser extent, was piracy. In fact a tombstone in the parish church, dated 1635, records the sad outcome of one such event.

But perhaps one of Ilfracombe's most enigmatic stories concerns the discovery in the last century of a woman's skeleton within a sealed room at Chambercombe Manor. The manor had long enjoyed a reputation for being used by both wreckers and smugglers and it was allegedly here that the gangs had their headquarters. Locals believed that they had access to the sea through a hidden tunnel which led from Chambercombe to nearby Hele Bay. As to the body of the young woman found secreted there, speculation is all that one can offer. Some say the body was that of the daughter of the wreckers' leader, who had somehow displeased her father and had been walled-up to starve as punishment. However, another school of thought is that it was the body of a young Spanish girl who was caught after the vessel on which she was sailing was lured ashore by the wreckers. It is another case where we shall never know the truth.

One previous occupant of Chambercombe Manor of whom we do have a record was Lady Jane Gray. A tragic young girl who lived only seventeen years, between 1537–1554, she is best known for her short reign as Queen of England after the death of Edward VI. It lasted only nine days before she was deposed and executed by Mary Tudor.

In policework there is always the unexpected. The Ilfracombe case of the legless corpse is a good example of things which are not always what they first seem. This case occurred in Ilfracombe in the nineteen sixties and the investigation started when strollers in Bicclescombe Park found a legless body in the small stream which runs through this popular playground.

Hurrying to the scene the police officers indeed confirmed that the facts were as reported. The body was of an elderly man, poorly dressed and probably a tramp. He was legless and had undoubtedly drowned. A search of the scene was made as a matter of routine and it was not long before material evidence came to light. Further upstream police officers found two artificial limbs stuck fast in the mud! It seems that apparently the tramp went to the stream for some reason but got stuck. In releasing his limbs he lost his balance, falling into deeper water where he drowned. It was a case of bad luck.

Lundy
Land of Pirates and Puffins

Stand on almost any high ground along the north Devon coast and look westwards and you will see a part of the County which police officers virtually never visit. At any rate certainly not on duty. It lies some twenty-three miles from Ilfracombe and at its nearest point to land is twelve miles north-west of Hartland

Point. I refer to the Island of Lundy. Ilfracombe used to be the main port for access to the island although in recent years this has become a seasonal service only. The main link has now been switched to Bideford with regular crossings by the *M.V. Oldenburg,* a 300 tonne vessel which carries over 250 passengers in addition to cargo for the island.

Lundy rises high out of the rough Atlantic waters as though it were a sentinel guarding the entrance to the Bristol Channel. Its four hundred foot cliffs are frequently storm-lashed and the two-hour sea crossing is not for the poor sailor. Whilst I admit to never having set foot on Lundy, as a young police officer at Bideford a colleague and I used   occasionally to spend our weekly rest day helping one of the local trawler owners fish the grounds off the island. That was an experience in itself ... we netted a young shark once!

The island has a long history of lawlessness which fortunately does not prevail today. Early records show that it was occupied in the thirteenth century by a William de Marisco. He was reputed to have been of noble birth but became styled as the 'Pirate King of Lundy.' After his death his family continued to 'rule' the island. Eventually it fell to the Crown but has since had many private owners. When it was purchased by the Harman family in 1925, Martin Cole Harman tried to run it as a private kingdom but some years later fell foul of the Law of Westminster when he introduced his own currency. This was named after some of Lundy's most celebrated inhabitants ... the Puffin. I am proud to be the owner of postage stamps based on this illegal currency although I hasten to add they are of no monetary value.

Today the island is owned by the National Trust but is administered and financed by the Landmark Trust on their behalf. There are a number of holiday cottages on the island, the scant remains of the thirteenth century castle of the Marisco's and the nineteenth century church, all situated at the southern end. But perhaps the most favourite port of call is to the aptly named Marisco Tavern where even today normal rules do not seem to apply.

Lynton & Lynmouth

The Floods That Destroyed the Village.

I cannot leave North Devon, however, without mention of the last town to be policed by the local Force before the boundary is reached with Somerset. I refer, of course, to the twin resorts of Lynton and Lynmouth. It was here, in 1952, that one of the greatest natural disasters ever to hit the country occurred ... the Lynmouth floods.

The problem started on Friday, 15th August, when over nine inches of rain fell on Exmoor in less than twenty-four hours. In fact rainfall records show that six inches of this fell within only five hours. It is but a short distance to Lynmouth from the Moor and two of the main rivers, the East and West Lyn, converge on the outskirts of the town to form a common exit to the sea. Both rivers are fed by countless small tributaries, one of the larger being the Hoar Oak Water. In no time at all they became swollen and the force of the torrent was greatly increased by the fact that initially the flow was constrained by steep and narrow gorges. As the force of water grew, and levels rose, the spate began to dislodge boulders and trees from the rivers' banks and carry them along in its path. Some of the boulders were later estimated to have weighed in excess of twenty-five tons. Soon both trees and boulders were piling up under bridges, causing the waters to rise even further. Finally they burst their banks and a wall of water and debris hit the town. Within seconds Lynmouth was uninhabitable.

Police records show that thirty-four persons died, many swept out to sea, and one hundred and eighty two properties were either completely destroyed at the time or later found to be damaged to such an extent that they were beyond repair. In addition ninety-four vehicles were swept straight out to sea whilst a further seventy-five were submerged under water within the town. Nineteen vessels moored in Lynmouth's small harbour were also swept away and disappeared.

Much has been written elsewhere about this disaster and today there is a small museum in Lynmouth which records this tragic episode in their history. It is hoped that flood prevention schemes initiated during the architecturally sympathetic rebuilding of the town will prevent any such occurrence happening again. I cannot leave this event, however, without some comment on the problems often faced by 'the thin blue line'.

In 1952 the official police establishment for the area was one Sergeant and three Constables stationed at Lynton. A further two Constables were in detached beats, i.e. village stations, in the outlying countryside. These officers not only covered Lynton and Lynmouth, a very popular holiday area, but over a hundred square miles of other territory. On the fateful day the Sergeant was away from the area enjoying part of his annual leave and the senior constable, who deputised in his absence, was also off-duty on his statutory one rest day per week. In Lynton, therefore, the police contingent comprised a Constable with six years' service and a probationer with under two years. Fortunately on the night in question the senior constable was resting at home so was able to return to duty when the emergency arose.

As the storm leading to the floods worsened, and with it an increase in water level, so fear amongst the local inhabitants rose also. Ironically, it was probably this sense of foreboding which was to save many lives. Unable to sleep they remained out of bed and fully dressed. Throughout the evening problems for Lynmouth were mounting up. Significantly at seven-thirty in the evening all the electricity failed and from then on the only illumination in the town came from the constant flashes of lightning which dominated the otherwise ink-black sky. Two hours later, at nine-thirty, the town's two fire engines were sent to answer emergency calls from farmers who were reporting flooding at their premises. Both vehicles quickly became victims of the rising water and one was not retrieved until a week after the floods had subsided.

In the meanwhile the police officers enlisted the help of the remaining firemen, the local doctor and other townspeople to organise rescue parties. As the situation deteriorated so help was being mobilised outside the area. Sources of extra manpower came from the Army and the Royal Air Force as well as the Police themselves. The first outside help managed to get through to the stricken area at two o'clock in the morning but they were the last for a further seven hours. For that period both Lynton and Lynmouth became completely cut off from the outside world.

Police records show the enormity of the communications problem which existed. A total of sixteen bridges altogether were swept away and a further fourteen road bridges were badly damaged. In addition, nineteen roads, including the main 'A' class road which carried the bulk of the traffic, were all made impassable.

There were many awards made for the bravery displayed that night and amongst the recipients were the three local constables. One received the George Medal and the other two the British Empire Medal.

Today, over forty years on, Lynmouth shows few scars of its past. In the upper reaches of Hoar Oak Water and the East Lyn River, which once brought so much destruction, otters now breed. And in Lynton's Valley of the Rocks the Peregrine Falcon has returned to grace the skies. For the moment nature seems at peace.

John 'Babbacombe' Lee - ' The man they could not hang'

Chapter 3
Torbay

Torquay:
The Man Who Would Not Hang
The Murder Of P.C. Smith
The Oil Threat

Teignmouth: *The French Connection*

Bishopsteignton: *Bishop's Holiday Home & Cock Fighting*

Newton Abbot: *Puritan Preachers & Political Riots*

Denbury: *The Missing Harleys*

Ashburton: *Roundheads & Raving Loonies*

Paignton: *Chiming Clock & Haunted Police Station*

The end of 1954 saw another posting and my departure from Bideford. As a result I duly reported for duty at Torquay Police Station with all my worldly possessions packed in the back of my pre-war Morris '8' 2-seater tourer. For a young police officer the difference between North and South Devon could not have been more pronounced. Here, at Torquay, working the late shift was no encumbrance to a full social life. With the shift ending at 10 p.m. this was the time when the former '400' Club and the Spa Ballroom were coming to life!

I was, however, to see Torquay in a different light when I returned to the area again in 1970. Officially my posting was to Paignton as sub-divisional Inspector but the organisation of duties meant that about every six seeks I had overnight responsibility for the policing of the whole Torbay Division. This not only included Torquay and Paignton but also Brixham, Newton Abbot, Teignmouth and Dawlish, an area with a population approaching a quarter of a million sleeping souls. It was also a time that, whilst visiting the night patrol officers at these stations, I learnt more unusual facts about the area we were policing.

Torquay
The Man Who Would Not Hang

There is probably no more unusual event in British criminal history than that concerning the Torquay case of John Henry George Lee. Lee was born in 1864 at Abbotskerswell, about five miles from Torquay. His first job, around 1879, was in the home of a Miss Emma Keyse. She was a woman of limited independent means who had once been in the service of Queen Victoria. She was well respected locally and lived in a large house, The Glen, which stood in a superb spot only yards from the beach at Babbacombe. Lee's employment lasted only twelve months after which he left to join the Royal Navy. Unfortunately for him he was invalided out a couple of years later. He returned to the Babbacombe area of Torquay and quickly found fresh work, none of the positions lasting long. On the last occasion his employer found him stealing and as a result Lee served six months in Exeter prison.

On his release his first employer, Miss Keyse, took pity on him and offered him another job as her handyman. Everything went well for the first few months but then Lee began to slack at his work. He paid no heed to warnings from his employer but, as she didn't want to turn him out onto the streets, she deducted money from his wages to cover his loss of productivity. There is no doubt that arguments ensued following this course of action and that these led to the fateful night on Saturday, 15th November 1884.

Miss Keyse went to bed as normal. In the middle of the night, however, her cook, an Elizabeth Harris who happened to be a half-sister to Lee, smelt smoke and raised the alarm. On making her way downstairs she came across the body of Miss Keyse lying on the floor of the dining room. Her body was partly burnt and lying near by were remains of newspapers which had been soaked in paraffin.

The initial police investigation showed that Miss Keyse's throat had been cut and her skull fractured. A bloodstained axe was found near the body and the use of paraffin to accelerate the burning was substantiated. When Lee appeared with injuries to his arm and unable to give a satisfactory account as to how they were caused or to his whereabouts at the material time, he was arrested and charged with murder. Mr Justice Manisty passed sentence of death on Lee at Exeter on the 4th February 1885 with the execution fixed for the 23rd of that month.

What happened next has been the subject of speculation for over a hundred years. At the appointed hour Lee approached the scaffold. All the preparatory work had been carried out and the tests showed that the equipment functioned correctly. The hangman, Mr James Berry, pinioned Lee's arms and led him towards the fatal retribution. The noose around Lee's neck, Berry pulled the lever which would drop Lee's body to the void below, breaking the neck in the process. Nothing happened. Tests were carried out and the scaffold worked properly. Lee was again placed over the trapdoors and the lever pulled. Again nothing happened. Lee was led away whilst yet more tests were carried out. Using sacks the same weight as Lee, the trap worked perfectly. Lee was brought back and Berry made his third attempt to carry out the execution. The result was the same as on the other occasions. The trap stayed shut. At this the prison chaplain, the Rev. John Petkin, instructed that the execution be postponed. Lee was subsequently reprieved by the Home Secretary and a sentence of Life imprisonment imposed instead. He was finally released on 18th December 1907. He briefly returned to Abbotskerswell where he married a nurse from the local workhouse before leaving the area for good.

What saved John Lee? Was it luck or divine intervention? Or was it sabotage? A number of explanations have been put forward although Lee, himself, had apparently predicted he would not hang. Berry, the executioner, blamed the design of the trap although it had worked in practice. Then it was suggested that heavy overnight rain had caused the timbers to swell although, in his report, Berry says a warder brought him an axe and a plane and they cut a corner of the wood. The most plausible solution I have heard came years later and is attributed to one of the warders who had been present when Lee walked to the scaffold. It appears that in those days the scaffold was built within the prison by convict labour. In Lee's case it was built by a 'lifer' who had been a master joiner before his prison sentence and it was his 'expertise' which was to give rise to the sensational events which occurred.

The carpenter realised that, at the time of execution, the prison's padre always stood in front of the condemned man on the scaffold. He therefore constructed it in such a way that it was not the trap which could be found at fault but a board on which the padre stood. This had been cut in such a way as to jam the hatch at the appropriate moment. Of course the padre's natural reaction as soon as the scaffold failed was to move from the spot and thus no fault was found. A plausible story? ... again this is one of those mysteries where we shall never know the truth!

Policing Torbay, and Torquay in particular, has never been easy. Whilst the resident population's age is above average, the summer sees a huge influx of younger visitors drawn to the area by its sunshine record, plenty of reasonably-priced accommodation and a night-life to suit most tastes. The numerous bars, discos and clubs often give rise to drink - and, to a lesser extent, drug-related offences.

The question I ask is ... is it any worse now? Many will probably say that it is, but I wonder. In the early 19th century Torquay had its own police force and records show that, by 1841, it had a 'Chief Constable' and six untrained assistants. Five years later, in 1846, a report shows that there was a concerted campaign against the inefficiency of the Force, led by a local newspaper. Apparently the total annual expenditure of policing the borough was only £179, with weekly pay being sixteen shillings (£0.80). The fact there had been a spate of local burglaries at the time probably did not help the public's confidence.

Compared with other South Devon resorts such as Exmouth, Sidmouth and Teignmouth, Torquay was a very late developer and only expanded to cater for the Victorian holiday trade once communications improved beyond Exeter. However, by the mid-nineteenth century, it was beginning to show signs of a life which did not please everyone as an 1853 report to the local magistrates reveals. In it the Chief Constable complained of the "unbecoming manner in which young women of the town wander around the thoroughfares without bonnets and shawls," and he asked the magistrates for advice on how he should deal with the problem. He was told that he already had the powers to bring before the court persons of such character who are "in any way indecent or guilty of unbecoming behaviour."

Fortunately for Torquay its archaic force came to an end after the passing of the County Police Act, 1856. On the 25th November, 1856, the Devon County Constabulary was formed and early the following year took over responsibility for policing Torquay. Eight trained Constables were immediately appointed. A new police station was opened in Market Street in 1871 and the building still stands. However this was vacated by the Force in 1944 when a new headquarters was built for them at Torre. These premises are still in use today.

However, despite the fact that the new Force was a 'trained' one, the general ignorance of those early police officers did not seem to improve immediately after the County Constabulary took over. This is graphically illustrated by an account of a discipline offence published in Chief Constable's Orders dated July 1869. This read as follows; "A first class Constable stationed at Torquay, 'F" Division, having shewn the most disgraceful ignorance of his duty, in having taken into custody and locked up a servant girl, who was charged by her master 'with refusing to go to bed when requested to do so' he, the said Constable, is reduced to the rank of 2nd Class ... but for his general good character this Constable would have been dismissed the Force for shewing an ignorance of duty that would be a disgrace to a recruit of six months standing."

Fortunately things are much improved today but, even so, Torquay was not lagging when it came to innovative matters. A memorandum to Quarter Sessions, dated 4th January 1887, reports that the Torquay police station was the first in the Force to be connected to the telephone service. The local telephone company had agreed to install the equipment free of charge subject to the police paying the subsequent rental fees.

The Murder of P.C. Smith

In an earlier chapter I mentioned the murder of P.C. Potter at Whimple but danger for police officers is ever present as the tragic events of a December night in 1973 show only too well.

On this fateful night Constable Dennis Smith, a 44-year-old family man, was on mobile duties within the Torquay area. It was only three days before Christmas and no doubt he was thinking about the joys of the festivities which lay ahead. But his mind was alert also to the responsibilities of his job and when he spotted a car being driven erratically he radioed to control that he was in pursuit through a residential part of Torquay. As the vehicles came down towards the harbour the offending vehicle suddenly pulled off the main road and stopped. The officer got out of the police car and approached the driver but, as he did so, the offender leapt out of his vehicle and opened fire with a handgun. When other officers arrived at the scene they found Dennis Smith lying bleeding behind the abandoned vehicle. He had died instantly from gunshot wounds. The police car was missing.

But that was not the end of the carnage. Only minutes later the same gunman burst into a casino in Torwood Street which was filled with gamblers enjoying a pre-Christmas spree. He opened fire at random and three more innocent victims fell dead, with a further two injured, in the hail of bullets.

Needless to say, a full-scale police manhunt followed with check-points quickly being organised on all the main roads. The murderer had not reckoned on the vigilance of police officers who, in the early hours of the following morning, saw a van under suspicious circumstances on the outskirts of Exeter. A high-speed chase followed with the vehicle finally being stopped at Newton Poppleford. The driver was quickly overpowered and arrested by three officers. There were two loaded revolvers on the seat beside the driver. The police officers were unarmed.

In another similar gun incident the unfortunate victims were the staff of the Social Security Offices in Abbey Road, Torquay.

A very disgruntled, and disturbed, customer entered their offices and began indiscriminate firing with a shotgun. Five members of the staff fell dead or seriously wounded. This was a period in the policing history of Torquay when the Chief Constable had to report that there had been more murders inflicted by firearms in Torquay during the year than the whole of the Metropolitan Police District.

Oil Threat

For enthusiasts of things maritime, Torbay will be a seventh heaven. I must admit, however, that local councillors do not always view the frequent proliferation of shipping in the bay in a similar light. The bay has long been recognised as a safe anchorage and many has been the occasion during winter storms that I have seen over thirty vessels of varying tonnage sheltering from the rougher waters of the English Channel. But it is not this aspect which gives rise to local anxieties but the more recent practice of off-shore oil transference from the gigantic super-tankers to smaller vessels capable of entering a wider selection of ports. To date there have been no mishaps but disaster plans for an oil spillage are always kept ready.

One near disaster occurred in the early hours of a summer morning in 1971 whilst I was the duty Inspector. A tanker, the *M.V. Trinity Navigator,* laden with crude oil and operating with a Chinese captain and foreign-speaking crew under a flag of convenience, for no conceivable reason came too close to the rocks beneath Berry Head at Brixham and ran aground. It was a period of spring tides and the morning tide was about an hour off peak. The police and local authorities were informed and relevant staff were put on standby to commence a massive oil spillage clean-up operation if the worst happened. Communications with Berry Head were essential so, together with other police officers, I went to the scene where already a large crowd of onlookers were gathering. I can only describe the next two hours as being somewhat nerve-racking.

The hero of the hour was the local Brixham pilot, Captain Bob Curtis. He quickly boarded the stricken tanker and immediately made his way to the bridge where he took control. The tide was already peaking and within a couple of hours would have dropped too far for refloating to be possible. At that point the weight of the cargo would most likely break the ship's back on the rocks and twenty thousand tonnes of crude oil would creep towards the beaches of Torbay. But the pilot wasn't to be beaten. For over an hour he coaxed the stricken vessel's propellers. First the stern, then the bow and side thrusters, each time inching the huge ship one way or another. Gasps came from the large crowd of onlookers, who had massed on the cliffs at Berry Head above the vessel, every time her steel-plated hull scraped, groaning across the rocks hidden beneath the surface. Slowly she inched off and with less than fifteen minutes to spare she was afloat in the bay.

I understand that in the enquiry which followed it was found that the ship's navigational equipment was faulty and this was exacerbated by the fact that the crew were asleep at the time with nobody on watch.

This was not the first time, however, that I had reason to be thankful for Captain Curtis's great seafaring skills. We had met earlier in the winter during one of those winter storms when countless ships were sheltering from the severe gale force winds. The police had received an SOS call from one of the vessels lying offshore. As I recall she was taking a cargo from Germany to the Argentine and sailing with a Dutch captain and a motley, mainly Asiatic, crew. Trouble had flared on board after a row over the food with the result that the cook had been stabbed and the offender had been locked in a cabin. The captain was now requesting a doctor and the police. In Brixham I picked up the local police surgeon and the Sergeant before going to the pilot cutter. The next quarter of an hour was like an eternity as the small craft pitched and tossed through huge seas and a howling gale. The light on the vessel we were making for never seemed to get any nearer, and, when it finally did, I almost wished it hadn't. The ship seemed a monster when viewed from the small pilot cutter alongside. A rope ladder was thrown over the side for us to climb but the gap between us and the ship's side seemed to vary from second to second, first three feet then ten! Only the great skill of the pilot prevented a collision and, at the same time, kept us close enough to board.

The cook's wounds were not life-threatening and, after treatment, he opted to stay aboard. As for the offender, he turned out to be a mild sort of character whom one would not normally think capable of violence. Nevertheless the captain refused to keep him on board and it became one of those occasions when I wished I had studied the Merchant Shipping Acts a little more closely. At the end of the day, however, it was common sense which prevailed. We took the offender ashore and boarded him in the cells for the rest of the night. The following morning he was released, without being criminally charged, to the care of one of the Shipping Agents.

Visitors to Berry Head today will find plenty of material to read on the Napoleonic fortifications, the lighthouse and the flora and fauna. The tourist literature does not mention, however, the small brick building which stands derelict and ivy-covered on the cliff edge a few hundred yards before the point. This is one of the last surviving examples of a second World War post which was manned by members of the Royal Observer Corps. A few yards away, to the right of the path leading to the lighthouse, the underground nuclear reporting post used post war by the same Corps now lies abandoned, one of the first casualties of the 1990's peace dividend.

Teignmouth
The French Visit!

Only six miles along the coast, north-east of Torquay, lies Teignmouth. Unlike its larger neighbour, Teignmouth has a long and interesting maritime history. It is known to have been a flourishing port as long ago as 1317 for in that year there is a record of a Teignmouth vessel, *La Redecoge,* delivering a cargo to Dublin. By the late sixteenth century Teignmouth men formed a large proportion of the fleet which fished for cod in the stormy North Atlantic waters off Newfoundland. A commentator of the day reported that the coast of Newfoundland was only half-ruled in a rough sort of way by the reckless valour of the Devonshire men, half traders, half pirates. Many of them maintained two families, one to provide comfort in the icy wastes, the other at home in Devon. Even today, a stretch of the coast outside Teignmouth is known as Labrador. However their dare-devil exploits earned them few friends amongst the other nations fishing the waters, particularly the French.

It is said that true natives of Teignmouth harbour strong feelings against the French which, in these more enlightened days of European harmony, is a pity. But when one looks at history the student may well be able to say they have a point.

For the record we have to look at events which occurred just over three hundred years ago, in 1690. William, Prince of Orange, had landed at nearby Brixham, stopped briefly at Newton Abbot and then gone on to London to claim the throne of England. James II had fled to France where he persuaded the French fleet to sail against the English. They did ... and won. Flushed by this unexpected success they sailed down the channel and eventually anchored off Teignmouth. The town certainly looked prosperous. It was overlooked by an impressive church and had a fine harbour with, no doubt, packed warehouses. But above all they remembered the reputation Teignmouth men had gained whilst sailing in Newfoundland waters and here was a chance to settle old scores. After waiting for a few days off-shore, they sailed in and put the town to the torch.

As the raiding parties came so the locals fled to the safety of the Haldon Hills where they lit signal beacons. Help came but it was too late. The French had pulled out and as they sailed up the channel all that was left of Teignmouth was a smoking ruin. This was, I believe, the last invasion of mainland Britain by foreign troops. Today, in aptly named French Street, a small plaque commemorates the 'visit' of our near neighbours.

With the closure of Exmouth docks, Teignmouth has become busier than ever and is now probably the busiest port in the County, with the possible exception of Plymouth. But the amount of shipping also gives rise to other problems, particularly when pleasure craft are also taken into account. Teignmouth has always had a reputation for smuggling and boasts a 'genuine' smugglers' tunnel the other side of the river at Shaldon. Here a tunnel cut through the dark red sandstone runs from the Ness to a small sandy beach below the headland.

Traditions often run deep and here they are no exception. During the nineteen eighties combined operations by both customs officers and the police have netted substantial hauls of contraband which have included both cigarettes and drugs.

Bishopsteignton
Bishops' Holiday Home and Cock-Fighting

A couple of miles from Teignmouth, facing the upper Teign Estuary, lies the village of Bishopsteignton. It is a quiet village which once enjoyed far greater importance than it does today. For, as the name suggests, this is where the Bishops of Exeter used to have their summer palace. Now only scant remains of a few walls are left. Interestingly, it is here that a few of the older locals still remember stories of the police raid which occurred one Monday afternoon on a barn in the nearby hamlet of Luton. Full details, and a lurid description of the evidence found by the two police constables, were given prominence in the local press. The crime: cock fighting. The date: 1877. In this particular case the evidence was in fact handed over to an Inspector of the R.S.P.C.A. which shows that, they too, were doing good work over a century ago.

Newton Abbot
Puritan Preachers & Political Riots

At the head of the Teign estuary lies Newton Abbot, a busy market town. Forde House, which now houses the District Council Offices, dates from the sixteenth century and was the first stop made by William, Prince of Orange, after his landing at Brixham. His first night's rest was spent here. Local folklore maintains that there is a long tunnel running under the town from the house to Bradley Woods which formed an escape route for Royalist sympathisers during the Civil War. It is on the outskirts of these woods where one will find the town's other link to the past, the small mediaeval manor house known as Bradley Manor. It is still occupied but now owned by the National Trust. Visits are possible on certain days of the year.

Also nearby, in the woods, is Puritans' Pit which has been described geologically as a collapsed limestone cavern. In the seventeenth century, a local Puritan minister, a William Yeo, regularly preached here at night after being ejected from his own church for refusing to accept the Act of Uniformity. Although there was a price on his head of two pounds he was never betrayed and died around 1699 at the ripe old age of eighty-two.

Seeing the town today it is hard to imagine that strong political feelings could cause a problem, particularly with local farmers more likely to be interested in the price of livestock in the market than the state of the Government. But that was not always the case.

In January, 1908, rioting broke out in the town during a parliamentary election for the mid-Devon, or Ashburton, constituency. Newton Abbot was a Liberal stronghold but the promotion of the sitting member to the High Court meant a by-election had to be held. Spice was added to the campaign when the veteran suffragette, Mrs Pankhurst, together with her daughter and another woman, allied themselves to the Conservative cause.

The result was a shock for the Liberals. They lost by the narrow margin of 559 votes and immediately blamed the interference of 'outsiders', namely the suffragettes, for their defeat. When Mrs Pankhurst and her friends appeared, the mob, set on vengeance, turned on them and the women had to flee. With the mob in pursuit they took shelter in a shop but worse was to come.

Shortly afterwards a Superintendent arrived from Torquay with a number of police officers. But the mob turned on them, pelting the officers with rotten eggs and tearing the Superintendent's tunic from his back. The crowd made clear its intentions were to throw the women into the River Lemon which runs through the town. Eventually the police were able to get the women away by car but not before Mrs Pankhurst had been knocked to the ground and trampled upon.

With the departure of the women the mob turned their attentions elsewhere. Their target was the Conservative Club in Union Street which, ironically, stood on the other side of the road to the Liberal Club. Any loose object which could be found was hurled at the building with the result that practically every window was smashed. Persons wearing Conservative colour rosettes were immediately attacked.

Eventually the Chief Constable himself, appeared on horseback leading a contingent of mounted officers to augment the hundred who were already present on foot. Two magistrates were called and asked to read the Riot Act thus giving the police added powers to clear the streets. They refused and went home. As darkness fell the situation deteriorated further and the police, under orders, remained comparatively inactive. This changed, however, just after midnight when one officer was severely attacked by the mob. Frustration gave way to positive response and following a sharp police assault the mob retreated and went home.

The fury of the mob can be best illustrated, however, by the tragic discovery the following day of Sergeant Major Reynell in the Town Mill Leat. It was known he was a staunch Conservative supporter. His body had been battered and foul play was suspected but nobody was ever brought to trial and the coroner's jury recorded an open verdict.

Denbury

The Man Who Crowned King William & The Missing Harleys

More recent events have given rise to a mystery at the nearby small village of Denbury. In fact the village has a history older than its mother town. There is some evidence of an original Saxon settlement which was fortified by a hilltop camp. Apparently its priest was a man called Aldred whom it is said rose to become Archbishop and one of the most powerful men in the land. Not only did he crown the last of the Saxon kings, King Harold, but also crowned the first Norman king of England, King William.

Level ground near the village was also chosen for the County's first airfield in the 1920s. It flourished for a few years with visits by various 'barnstormers' and a small airline, Provincial Airways, operated from here for a while. Eventually it seems to have lost out to the airfield at Haldon which is mentioned later.

Even though the aircraft left, the site did not become useless and it was here, during World War II, that the U.S. Army established a large camp. It was a period when racial segregation could be seen at its worst with black troops only being allowed into town one day a week when white troops were kept in camp for the day. It was the eventual departure of the American forces which has given rise to speculation amongst the villagers and I am indebted to one of our Special Constables for telling me the story. It appears that amongst equipment stored at the camp was a large number of Harley Davison motorcycles, brand new and still in their crates. Of no further use to the departing forces, the motorcycles and an amount of other equipment were buried on the camp. Fact or fiction? I have heard other similar stories but none of equipment being found! Should you feel like visiting the area with a metal detector, forget it, the site is now the home of Channings Wood prison.

Ashburton
Roundheads and Raving Loonies

Ashburton, six miles from Newton Abbot and one of the ancient stannary towns, has held a market since at least the twelfth century. Other links to the past will be found in the town which include the ironmonger's shop on the corner of North Street. These premises were used for a short period during the Civil War as a Headquarters by parliamentarian forces under General Fairfax. They were more comfortable in those days being then known as the Mermaid Inn.

More recently, Ashburton has made national prominence for its more unusual political leanings. Politics, however, have always been of interest in the town and the riots which occurred in Newton Abbot in 1908 basically concerned the local constituency. The town's Golden Lion Hotel, built in 1768 and formerly a coaching inn, features strongly in these stories.

One of the earlier landlords was a William Baron who took up occupancy around 1825. He was a die-hard Tory and apparently recruited local rabble to intimidate the voters into following his persuasion, or at least abstaining. Matters came to a head, however, in 1837 when this so-called private army abducted a prominent local Liberal and a full scale riot broke out.

Today the Golden Lion still basks in political importance. In 1990 the hotel became the official headquarters of the Monster Raving Looney Party and its landlord, Alan Hope, had the distinction of being the first member of that party ever to be elected to a position of civic trust when he became a member of the Town Council.

Paignton
The Chiming Clock & Haunted Police Station

Finally I return to Paignton, the middle of the three towns which make up the modern Borough of Torbay and where I was stationed for a short period in the early 'seventies. Firmly on the tourist map with its busy beach of reddish sand, small harbour and impressive Oldway Mansion, which was built by a member of the Singer family and is now owned by the local authority.

It would be naive to say that Paignton is crime-free because it is not. But very often it is the simple cases which are the most interesting. Take, for instance, the case of the chiming clock. One of my colleagues, a detective Constable in the town, was called to the home of two old spinsters who had been visited by a couple of shady antique dealers. Nothing had been stolen but he interviewed them with a view to getting descriptions and other relevant information. They were pleased to have company and perhaps kept him talking longer than normal. Once particular thing he noticed was the chiming clock, mainly because it chimed on the quarter hour and always seemed to interrupt him when he was coming to a salient point. Eventually he left and would process the information he had been given. Unfortunately the 'dealers' returned the following day and stole a number of items, including the clock.

On the second occasion, however, one of the neighbours had seen their vehicle and remembered the number. A computer check quickly revealed the owner and the officer went to an address. The dealer denied all knowledge of the theft but stated he and a colleague had been legitimately canvassing in the area. No witnesses had seen them leaving the scene of the burglary and the officer was just about to leave the dealer's shop. Suddenly, from a room at the back, he heard a sound which so recently had been imprinted on his mind ... the chimes of the clock!

What has stuck foremost in my mind, however, is a bizarre incident which occurred one night in 1971 whilst I was the 'on duty' Inspector. I was in Torquay at the time but was quickly summoned, by radio, to return to Paignton. On my arrival I was told an incredible story.

The divisional police headquarters at Paignton was, at that time, a new building only recently having been commissioned. The second floor housed the canteen with quarters for police women above that. On the night in question a young Constable, who was on night duty, left the office about 2 a.m. to go to the canteen for his meal break. He never reached there.

As he walked along the second floor corridor towards the turning which would lead to the canteen he stopped abruptly in his tracks. Crossing the corridor in front of him drifted the form of a female dressed in a grey cloak. As suddenly as she had appeared she vanished through the wall. A sudden chill had accompanied this manifestation. Needless to say the young officer was badly shaken.

I am indebted, however, to the policewoman sergeant, later to be promoted to Inspector, who remained stationed at Paignton long after I left and who has furnished me with details of the past history of the site and of further manifestations which have occurred.

The new police station was apparently built on the site of a very old house which stood secluded behind high walls and was occupied by two old ladies who lived as virtual recluses. As one may expect as the property became more dilapidated, and the garden overgrown, local stories grew that the house was haunted. It was the sort of place that the paperboy scurried past. The ghost was reputed to be that of a servant girl. Certainly since the house was demolished, and the police station erected, a number of peculiar instances have occurred. In addition to the one I was aware of I have now learnt that one of my successors had an unusual experience. He was the late duty Inspector when he had occasion to go to the second floor of the building to use the photocopy machine. He had a considerable amount of copying to do and eventually had quite a pile of documents stacked by his side. Suddenly the whole pile rose into the air and blew around the room. There were no windows open, no draughts and no other person in sight.

A frightening experience also struck the police club's barman one night. He wanted to make a quick visit to his car which was parked in a side road near the police station. He took the shortest route, down the fire escape at the rear of the building. Just as he touched ground he felt an extreme chill and this was followed by an icy grip on his arm. There was nobody there. Alarmed at this experience he dashed back to the club where a number of witnesses would vouch to the fact that his arm shook uncontrollably and still felt cold to the touch. Other police officers have also experienced a sense of unease.

But that is not the end of the story. There is another bizarre twist. In the early 1980s it became necessary to rehouse the divisional control room which, until that time, had been situated in the front of the building on the ground floor. Increased use of technology, including in-house computer systems, rendered the original room too small and a decision was taken to re-locate it in larger, and more secure, premises on the top floor. It would be towards the rear of the building, the area where all the reputed sightings of the ghost had been.

At first everything seemed normal but after a while the Police National Computer V.D.U. screens seemed to go on the blink, the typewritten characters being replaced by snowy images. Each time the engineers from the Home Office Directorate of Telecommunications were called they could find no faults with the equipment. There were other occasions, usually at night, when electrical gadgets in the room would seemingly switch themselves 'on' and one officer swears he saw an electric switch on the wall move without being touched by human hand. Such occurrences have been confirmed by the Superintendent who, thinking electrical surges may have been the cause, had the whole system checked by electricians. They could find no electrical faults or any other cause of the phenomena. True … or imagination! It is yet another mystery we shall probably never solve.

Finally two animal stories about policing Paignton. The first was related to me by a local officer. It predates the above episode having occurred in the 1960s whilst the old police station in Palace Avenue was still in use. It is another story of the unexpected ... but with a different twist.

The events unfold with a telephone call being received at the police station of a large dog attacking other dogs in the park. Two young constables set off with a 'dog napper', a long pole with a noose on the end, and eventually located the offending animal. After a series of chases they managed to slip the noose over its head and with great difficulty brought it back to the police station where there was a kennel in the rear yard. But their troubles were not over. They could not put the restraining chain around the animal's neck so, in desperation, they put it in an empty cell.

Shortly afterwards the Sergeant returned from his meal break and, asking if anything had happened whilst he had been gone, one of the constables related the story of the dog and told him it was now in the cell. Apparently the Sergeant was none too pleased at this and told the young officers in no uncertain terms that cells were for people, kennels were for dogs and, furthermore, he would show him how to deal with stray dogs in future. It should be said at this point that the Sergeant was a big man. The Sergeant disappeared down the passage and entered the cell. For the next couple of minutes the constables heard a mixture of howls, swear words, yelps and bumps and then the Sergeant emerged from the cell. The animal lay over his shoulder, the head dangling down his back together with the fore-paws. One of his strong pair of hands held the hind paws in front of him whilst the other had a firm grip on the animal's testicles. Smiling broadly he told the young officers that was the way to deal with difficult dogs.

At that moment the telephone rang. The young constable answered it. It was Paignton Zoo. They were phoning to warn the police that they had lost one of their Siberian wolves ... I give you only one guess as to where it was at that moment!

A shaggy dog story? Well I must say there is no documentary evidence to support it but there is proof of an earlier escape from Paignton Zoo. This occurred in 1939 when a leopard attacked its keeper and made good its escape, inflicting severe wounds to the keeper in doing so. The police were informed and messages broadcast on the B.B.C. Troops from a local Anti-aircraft battery were put at the disposal of the police. There were 'sightings' of the leopard all over Paignton during the next couple of days. But it had never left the zoo and the discovery of six rare but dead sheep in the grounds alerted the army search party. Forty-two hours after escaping Ben the Leopard lay dead, shot through the heart by an army marksman.

*The Church at Peter Tavy, scene of the horrifying murder
of two young lovers in 1892*

Chapter 4
Dartmoor and its Environs

Dartmoor Prison: *Riots & Death In The Reservoir*

Tavistock: *Home Of Goosey Fair*

Peter Tavy: *Lovers Murdered Leaving Church*

Lydford: *Foul Prison & The Pillaging Gubbins Clan*

Okehampton: *Lady Howard & Her Coach Of Bones*

Sampford Courtney: *The Prayer Book Rebellion*

Spreyton: *Home Of Old Uncle Tom Cobley*

Chagford: *Roundheads, Murder & Ghosts*

Jay's Grave: *A Haunting Spot*

Widecombe: *The Devil's Visit*

Buckfastleigh: *Deep Caves & The Vampire Squire*

South Brent: *The Priest's Murder*

Across the Moor: *More Hauntings & Corpse In The Chest*

Moretonhampstead: *Murder & Mistaken Identity*

Moorland Pubs: *Watch Out For The Axeman*

There are few places in the country where one's imagination can run as wild as it can on Dartmoor. There are countless books which may be purchased from bookshops, or borrowed from libraries, which give graphic accounts of an area which has often been described as England's last wilderness. I don't know if I would go quite that far but parts are certainly very bleak.

In writing about Dartmoor it is so easy to describe places which have been featured many times before, such as Childe's Tomb, haunting Wistman's Wood and the inaccessible bog of Cranmere Pool. Not forgetting either the ghostly legends of the Devil's footprints at Poundsgate or the Hairy Hand at Spitchwick! I will try to stick, therefore, to those odd facts which I found interesting as a police officer. In addition to the Moor itself, much of which is beyond the scope of other than the seasoned walker, I shall also look at some of the events which have occurred in a few of the towns and villages on the fringe of the National Park.

I first became acquainted with Dartmoor whilst I was based briefly at Plympton early in 1956 as a member of our Traffic Department but a much greater understanding arose during 1961–62 when I was living at Tavistock. I was still a member of the Traffic Department and the Tavistock posting was always looked upon as one which provided a premier response for the gaol breaks from the prison at Princetown. There were two patrol cars based in the town, each with a crew of two. When not in use they were garaged at home. In effect they were on the road for only eight hours a day and we kept them for four years. Such was the 'bull' in those days that when they finally went for sale they were cleaner than when they arrived from the factory. Even the engine was 'Brassoed'! And for easy access to the Moor, our pair of houses were literally on the edge. If we forgot to shut the front gate the ponies were in the garden! Those were also the days when an escape from Dartmoor involved over a hundred men in the ensuing manhunt and checkpoints were maintained for a week or more. But then some of the most dangerous criminals in the country were serving their sentences at 'The Moor'. Today the prison has been downgraded, escapes are fewer and of those who do abscond, I deliberately say abscond and not escape, do so whilst released on home leave and fail to return. Police manhunts are very much a thing of the past and the traffic cars were redeployed from Tavistock many years ago.

Dartmoor Prison

One cannot mention Dartmoor, however, without saying something about the prison and its origins. I have read a description of Princetown as being a 'dismal little town built around the prison.' I would risk the local's wrath if I went along with this but it does get more than its share of rain in the summer and snow in the winter. Add to that the Dartmoor fogs and the cool winds one must expect when situated 1400 feet above sea level and I suppose that writer does have a point!

But it wasn't the weather conditions which, by themselves, prompted the prison to be built. The prisoners' welfare was not considered a factor in the choice of site only the economic prosperity of a local landowner, Sir Thomas Tyrwhitt. He was very friendly with the Prince Regent and enjoyed his backing for the proposal that a prison should be built there to replace the rotting prison ships moored in the River Tamar at Plymouth. For Tyrwhitt the prison would generate wealth for a part of his estate which otherwise would remain virtually worthless. So pleased was he when his plans were accepted that he named the town which sprung up around the Prison, Princetown, after his friend the Prince Regent.

Building began in 1806 and was completed in 1809 at a cost of £130,000. Its original use was to house French soldiers and sailors captured during the Napoleonic War, particularly those who were in the prison ships. The Latin inscription above the main gate, when translated, reads "Spare the Vanquished," not

"Abandon hope all ye who enter here" as so many people seem to think although, at the time, the latter may have been more appropriate.

The Prison population grew steadily and by 1813 had reached over eight thousand when American seamen who were seized during the Anglo-American War of 1812–14 were added to the French captives. When peace was declared with the Americans at Christmas, 1814, there was a dispute between governments as to who would pay for their repatriation. As a result the prisoners stayed put.

This inability of the respective governments to reach a solution eventually led to one of the darker episodes in the prison's history. The American prisoners became restless and a minor incident got blown out of all proportion. The Governor called out the troops and ordered them to fire on the prisoners in the yard. Seven prisoners were killed and over fifty seriously injured. It has been said, however, that the casualties would have been very much greater had it not been for the fact that many of the soldiers could not bear to fire at unarmed men and fired into the air instead of into the crowd as ordered. But conditions within the prison also left much to be desired and a further two hundred and eleven American servicemen were to die during their imprisonment of disease, deprivation and the cold.

The parish church at Princetown was largely constructed by American and French prisoners between 1810–1815 and many have their final resting place in a prison cemetery so many miles from home. It is one of the more unusual links we have with the United States, albeit a sad one. Nevertheless it is this historical connection which brings many American visitors to Princetown each year and to the church in particular.

At the end of the wars, and the repatriation of prisoners of war, the prison's use diminished. In 1850, however, its fortunes changed when it was turned into a convict prison. This is a role it has kept to this day, the only changes being in its classification within the prison service. For most of its life Dartmoor has been classified as a secure prison and one to which all the worst offenders were sent. It had a hard core of 'lifers' and those serving sentences for particularly brutal crimes. This is no longer the case. Society changes and so do the sophisticated requirements needed to provide absolute security for those convicted of terrorist crimes and other vile acts. The very location of Dartmoor, and the age of the prison, made its continued use as a Grade One prison untenable. Following the Mountbatten Report on prison security, therefore, Dartmoor Prison was downgraded.

Unrest frequently simmers beneath the surface in any penal institution and Dartmoor is no exception. There have been a number of disturbances over the years, the last serious one being in 1990 when one man died. All, bar one, have been handled successfully by the prison authorities before erupting into a full-scale riot stage. That occasion was in January 1932. Unrest had been simmering·for weeks over the state of the prison food. On the Sunday, whilst the men had assembled for church service in the prison chapel the Governor decided to address them on the matter but he was booed down. Only the intervention of the prison chaplain saved the day. But the seeds of an uprising had been sown. The following morning, on being marched to the Chapel, the prisoners rebelled. This time they were ready and many were armed with weapons they had made secretly in the prison workshops, others had pick handles, crowbars and spades. A bloody and destructive mutiny had begun.

The mob, now in full cry, marched to the administration block and demanded the release of all prisoners held in the punishment block, threatening to burn down the prison if their demands were not met. An Assistant Prison Commissioner, visiting from London, attempted to plead with the men but was immediately attacked. Only the efforts of one of the prisoners saved his life … an act subsequently rewarded by a reduction in sentence. Things were deteriorating fast. The mob had broken into the Governor's and other offices looting and setting fire to buildings. And to make sure they burned they destroyed the prison's fire-engine. By now armed warders had assumed positions on the walls of the prison but there appeared to be no attempt at a mass break-out. When two prisoners climbed onto the roof of the twine shed they were shot by the warders. This action may have had a sobering effect on whether or not to charge the walls.

The end of the mutiny has been described as an anti-climax. Police were quickly mobilised from the neighbouring county stations and the City of Plymouth. The military also arrived. The police charged through the prison gates, truncheons at the ready. Skulls were cracked and the prisoners retreated to their cells. Had the police needed assistance the hundred armed troops waiting outside the gates would have been brought into action. Many prisoners received minor injuries during the baton charge but none of the police were hurt. The warders had not been so lucky and during the riot stage a number had been injured, one so badly he was subsequently invalided out of the service.

The conclusion to this episode in the prison's history came in April, 1932, when a special Court of Assize was held in Exeter. Thirty-three prisoners appeared before the Judge charged with offences ranging from attempted murder, causing bodily harm, rioting and wilful damage. Eleven were found 'not guilty' and acquitted. Punishments awarded to the remaining twenty-two ranged from an additional six months' imprisonment added to existing sentences to ten years' penal servitude.

During my period at Tavistock I was called out on a number of escapes. By far the majority of escapees were caught, and the odd few got away. On balance we usually won but whether the tremendous costs were worth it would be open to debate in today's financial climate. One escape in particular has always stuck in my mind because it created a mystery which was never solved. It was the escape of Denis Stafford, a Londoner convicted of a particularly brutal murder, who was serving a life sentence. In planning his escape he enlisted the help of another prisoner, called Day, and when the opportunity arose they made a break together. Stafford was never caught in this country but made news headlines a couple of years later when he was caught, and convicted, of the murder of a taxi driver whom he had shot and killed in Switzerland. He then faced a further life sentence after which he would be returned to serve the remainder of his British sentence. But what of his colleague Day? Well, he was found very much earlier - within a few weeks in fact - floating in Burrator Reservoir, one of the most-visited and scenic spots on the Moor. There was much speculation but the general consensus of opinion was that the poor man, having helped Stafford to escape, was of no further use to him and indeed had become an encumbrance. Stafford was a psychopathic killer so to him one more death would mean nothing but whether he was responsible for this one we shall never know.

Finally I must mention the prison break which occurred in 1966, at Christmas. Five inmates made good their escape but had not reckoned on the latest technology being available ... the helicopter. This was the first time a helicopter had ever been used by the former Devon Constabulary and was provided courtesy of the Army Air Corps. I was actually stationed at Exmouth, as Traffic Sergeant, at the time but my previous flying experience was quickly utilised and over the next six days I flew many hours in the tiny bubble-cockpitted Sioux. Although we did not personally apprehend any of the prisoners none of them managed to escape from the Moor. In the end they were glad to give up. The reason they all gave was fear of being spotted by the helicopter. Because of this they remained hidden all day and at night they were afraid to move because of the bogs!

Tavistock
Home of Goosey Fair

The principal town on the western edge of the Moor is Tavistock, small but attractive and the scene every year of a rather boisterous 'Goosey Fair'. The town can trace its origins back before the founding of its abbey in the twelfth century although little of this building remains. When the Abbey was surrendered to the newly appointed church commissioners of Henry VIII, the lands passed into the family of the Dukes of Bedford. Today one of the largest buildings in the town is the Bedford Hotel. This is centrally situated near Bedford Square where there are a number of attractive buildings of distinctive Victorian character.

One of these is the police station which is still being used as such after more than a hundred years. The former enquiry office lies below street level with a door approached by a number of stone steps. With the River Tavy nearby one disadvantage is rather obvious but is quaintly, and graphically, described in a police report of July 1890, and I quote:

"Sir, I have the honour to inform you that considerable damage has been done to Tavistock Police Station by the floods this morning. The water was 5ft. high in my office and in the cells and quarters. A prisoner had to be brought out of the cells when the water rose. The Sergeant and Constables barely had time to save their children. Some of the office books and nearly all the papers are rendered useless."

Peter Tavy
Lovers Murdered Leaving Church

Less than three miles north of Tavistock lies the small moorland village of Peter Tavy with its delightful country inn and fifteenth century church. If you visit the latter, pause by the Lych Gate for it was shortly after passing through here that two young lovers became victims of a murder which shook the small community. Although this case occurred in 1892 it was a scenario all too common today: ex-lover cannot come to terms with the situation so kills his former girl friend and her current boy friend. In this case the young couple, farmer's daughter Eunice Doidge, and a Frederick Rowe had just left church when they were confronted by the ex-boyfriend, Bill Williams. Two shots rang out. Eunice died instantly and Frederick a few hours later. Williams then turned the weapon on himself and onlookers saw a shot enter his neck before he leapt into the River Tavy. He was quickly pulled from the water and his life saved, albeit temporarily. He was subsequently tried for murder and found guilty. Four months later, in March 1893, he paid the ultimate penalty when he was hanged at Exeter. The police report shows that Williams had bought the fatal weapon from a Tavistock ironmonger's less than a week before.

Lydford

Foul Prison and the Pillaging Gubbins Clan

Further north of Tavistock, and roughly halfway between there and Okehampton, is the village of Lydford. To see it today belies the position it held in the Middle Ages when it was one of the most important Stannary Towns in the area although its history can be traced back to earlier Saxon and Norman times. It still regards itself as 'the Capital of Dartmoor' but could only justify it today by tradition. It does hold one record, however, in that it is the largest Parish in England albeit one with a very small population. One reminder of the harsh punishments inflicted on law breakers in days gone past will be seen at the Castle.

Lydford Castle, a gaunt stone edifice standing on a grassy mound, was principally used as a prison to hold those who offended against the ancient stannary laws of the tinners. Its reputation was awesome. Not only was it extremely damp and cold but it is said that once a prisoner was inside it was extremely rare for him to see daylight again. Even prisoners awaiting trial would spend a year or more in there before coming before the court, many dying before they could plead their innocence. A poignant reminder of those days can be found in the verses written in 1644 by a local poet, William Browne. I quote the first three lines of one.

> *I oft have heard of Lydford Law,*
> *How in the morn they hang and draw,*
> *And sit in judgement after.*

Today the twelth century keep is in the care of English Heritage and entry is free at any reasonable time.

More likely to be visited by tourists in the area is the famous

Lydford Gorge. This 1½ mile long gorge was fashioned by the River Lyd and provides a number of spectacles such as the hundred foot high White Lady Waterfall and the 'boiling' Devil's Cauldron. Today it is owned by the National Trust and persons entering there are warned of the potential dangers. Parts of the path underfoot can be very slippery in wet weather and to fall into some of the deep ravines through which the Lyd passes could have fatal consequences. But these dangers are minuscule to those faced by earlier travellers.

In the seventeenth century this was the haunt of the infamous Gubbins family. Thieves and outlaws, they feared neither man nor God. They lived in caves in inaccessible parts of the Gorge seemingly beyond the reach of the authorities. In fact it was not the law which finally put paid to their existence but their own life-style of gross intemperance and continual interbreeding.

Okehampton
Lady Howard and Her Coach of Bones

Progressing further north we come to Okehampton, the largest of the moorland fringe towns. A market town, it sits comfortably where the East and West Okement Rivers merge. It has a long history and its castle is well worth a visit.

Situated on the western edge of town, the County's largest castle stands in ruined splendour on a hill overlooking the gorge of the West Okement River. It is in the care of English Heritage and a personal stereo guide is available at the kiosk which gives a full commentary with a musical backing. Of Norman origin, it was considerably enlarged in the fourteenth century. One Victorian writer advised that the best time to visit was by moonlight although such advice should not be taken today. It may have been the legend of the castle which prompted him to pen those words.

Almost all old buildings are reputed to have their ghosts and Okehampton Castle is no exception. Here it is the ghost of Lady Howard of Fitzford who is doomed to haunt the castle for her misdeeds as an 'unnatural mother'. Legend has it that she sets forth from Tavistock on the nights of full moon in a coach of bones with the grinning skulls of her four husbands decorating each corner. It is preceded on its journey to Okehampton Castle by a jet black hound which, on each journey, takes one blade of grass from the castle mound back to Tavistock. When all the grass has gone then Lady Howard's soul will rest.

Sampford Courtney
The Prayer Book Rebellion

Although not strictly a moorland village, I feel Sampford Courtney which lies about four miles north-east of Okehampton is worthy of a short note to illustrate that even the smallest of places can precipitate events which have long-lasting consequences. It was here, in 1549, that the Prayer Book Rebellion broke out when the men of Devon refused to accept the new Prayer Book and assembled before marching to Exeter. The event occurred on Whit Sunday, the 9th June, when the new Prayer Book in English was introduced for the first time. The villagers forced the Priest to revert to the traditional Latin Mass. Local Justices intervened but the villagers would have none of this and promptly lynched one of them, a William Hellyons, on the steps of Church House which can still be seen today. The ensuing rebellion lasted over two months during which the old chancel was destroyed.

Spreyton
Home of Old Uncle Tom Cobley

Still proceeding around the Moor on its northern fringes we come to another small village, Spreyton. Whilst the story, and song, of Widecombe Fair and Tom Pearce's Grey Mare is well known, and indeed celebrated annually at Widecombe Fair, a fact which is less well-known is that Old Uncle Tom Cobley is reputed to have come from Spreyton. The local legend is evidenced by the fact there is a tombstone in the village churchyard dedicated to a Thomas Cobley who died in the nineteenth century aged 82 years. Perpetuating the story, the village inn is named after him. For those interested in the journey, Spreyton is about fourteen miles from Widecombe.

Continuing now towards the south-east we pass close to Castle Drogo which perches high above the gorge of the infant River Teign. It looks impressive, as indeed it is, but its only claim to historic importance is that it is the last castle to be built in the country. A masterpiece of the architectural genius of Sir Thomas Lutyens, it was built of granite between 1910–20. Today it is in the care of the National Trust. But our call is not to the castle but the nearby town of Chagford.

Chagford
Roundheads, Murder and Ghosts

Chagford is another moorland town with a long history, being one of the three original Stannary Towns with a charter granted in 1305. It was to here that the Dartmoor tinners would bring their metal for assay as to its purity, pay their taxes and then trade it to the merchants. A number of stone antiquities will be found on the moor close to the town but some of its buildings have an equally fascinating history.

First of these is the Three Crowns Hotel, a thatched inn, which was occupied in February 1643 by Parliamentarian Forces. In an attack by a Royalist contingent, a young Royalist was killed. He was a budding poet called Sidney Godolphin and by all accounts had packed much into his young life. Born at Godolphin in Cornwall in 1610 he was of noble birth. He went to Oxford at fourteen years of age and four years later was a Member of Parliament. Of pleasant disposition, he had acquired a reputation as a minor poet, a skill for which many thought he would eventually achieve fame. At the outbreak of the Civil War he returned to Cornwall to raise an army on behalf of the King. Unfortunately, en route, he became involved with the skirmish at Chagford and was shot dead in the porch of the inn. Today he lies at rest in the church at Okehampton, his young life coming to an end at the age of thirty-two.

Perhaps not so at rest is the body of poor Mary Whiddon. Again the Three Crowns features in the story which is set in 1641. Mary Whiddon was a local girl who, in 1641, married her sweetheart in the local parish church. After the ceremony the happy couple mingled with guests outside the inn. Unfortunately in the crowd was a former suitor who could not bear the thought of her with another man. He opened fire with a pistol and she fell dead. A stone slab in the floor of the church commemorates her death with the seemingly prophetic words, "Such damselles do not die but sleep." I say 'prophetic' because locals have been reported as seeing the ghost of a woman in black at Whiddon Park and this is where young Mary had lived.

Due south of Chagford lie two prehistoric settlements, Grimspound and Hound Tor. Both are shown on Ordnance Survey maps and make interesting visits for students of history, the latter being occupied as a homestead until climatic changes in the fourteenth century made further habitation untenable. But for another of the Moor's enigmatic stories we visit a spot on the lonely road which leads from the Hound Tor car park towards Chagford. At a point where a bridle path crosses the road lies Jay's Grave.

Jay's Grave
A Haunting Spot

Kitty Jay's story has formed part of local folklore for almost two hundred years. But like so many stories there are now differing versions. The most likely is that she was a young maid working at nearby Canna Farm who, when she found herself pregnant out of wedlock, hung herself from a beam in an outhouse.

Another source states that she was apprenticed from the Workhouse at Newton Abbot into service at Barracott Farm near Manaton. Instead of hanging herself one story says she drowned herself in a pond at the farm. The common these is, however, that she killed herself whilst facing the shame of pregnancy and the likelihood of being cast out, penniless, by her employer. The strict laws of the day prevented a suicide from being buried in consecrated ground to her young body was laid to rest at a quiet moorland spot.

Today the grave is still beside the road, a grassy mound flanked by granite kerbstones and sometimes topped by a simple wooden cross. One of the mysteries which surrounds it is the fact that it never appears to be without fresh flowers and yet no one is ever seen to be placing them there. However there have been reports of the ghostly form of a young lady being seen near the grave and this has given rise to local speculation that it is the ghost of Kitty herself who is responsible for putting the flowers there.

When I recently visited the site I found twigs had been placed on the top of the grave and from them hung votive offerings, probably left by the county or travelling folk who still regard the site with some awe. I have also heard from a colleague that some will not pass the site after dark. Is it really a grave the sceptics may ask? I honestly do not know but apparently there are records which show that in 1860 the grave was opened up and the skeleton of a young girl found. These also state that the bones were reburied on the same site. I am happy to leave it at that.

Widecombe In The Moor
The Devil's Visit.

Not so far from Jay's Grave, nestling in a valley below the high tors, lies Widecombe in the Moor. It is perhaps the most well-known of all the moorland towns, made even more so by the famous song 'Widecombe Fair' and Tom Pearce's grey mare! It is probably the most visited too and the annual fair held in

September attracts thousands, not only packing the village but all the approach roads as well ... a policeman's nightmare. The village police station disappeared in the reorganisations of the nineteen seventies and eighties but one of the village's former 'bobbies' deserves a mention if only to dispel a popular misconception about rural police officers. Because life is generally slower in the country many city visitors think the local bobby is also 'slow' and not so street wise as his rural counterpart. Wrong! My Widecombe colleague not only rose to high rank within the local Constabulary but went on to become Chief Constable of a major South Coast Force, President of the Association of Chief Police Officers and recipient of a Knighthood!

But to return to odd facts about Widecombe one must mention the Church of St Pancras, also known by locals as the 'Cathedral of the Moor'. It was originally built in the fourteenth century but enlarged a century later. The 120ft high tower, topped by four fine pinnacles, is one of the finest in the area and is said to have been built by tinners' money. It was one of these pinnacles which received the wrath of heaven on an October Sunday in 1638.

It was during the afternoon service when suddenly the day grew dark and an eerie blackness fell over the village. Equally suddenly there was a flash of light as a bolt of lightning hit one of the pinnacles on the tower, destroying it. But what happened inside the church at the same time takes some understanding. The power from the sky killed four of the church-goers and injured over sixty more. Reports say that some had their clothes burnt off them without harming their bodies. In trying to find an explanation for this tragedy the locals came to believe it was a visitation by the devil. On arrival Satan had tethered his horse to the pinnacle on the tower before entering the church. His mission? ... to claim the souls of one 'Widecombe Jan' and his colleagues who had showed their wickedness by playing cards at the back of the church instead of praying. An account of this visitation, in the form of a poem, is recorded within the church today.

Buckfastleigh

Deep Caves & the Vampire Squire

Coming south from Widecombe, across the moor on minor roads through Ponsworthy and Holne, Buckfastleigh is reached. This small town is today by-passed by the main Exeter to Plymouth dual-carriageway but nevertheless draws large numbers of visitors, mainly to the internationally-renowned abbey at neighbouring Buckfast. But one of Buckfastleigh's more interesting sites lays hidden from public gaze ... its unique caves.

Over a mile of caves, caverns and passages lie in the limestone rocks upon which the town is built. Many of the caverns have impressive stalactite formations. It has been recorded that over the years the cave system has yielded what has been perhaps the most comprehensive collection of bones of interglacial mammals yet to be found in Britain. Less encouraging for the archaeologist, however, has been the absence of any evidence of human habitation. Like all cave systems they can be dangerous although the Force has used those at Buckfastleigh in the past for the training of Police Cadets in caving techniques. Today they can be visited but the occasions are limited and it will be necessary to make local enquiries as to specific conditions and times.

Above ground, those who love an unusual tale should visit the Parish Church of Holy Trinity which stands high on a rock on the outskirts of the town. I visited it recently with a colleague who confirms the local story which concerns one Richard Cabell, the Squire of Brook Manor who died in 1677. He was, by all accounts, an evil man who had a reputation for pursuing local maidens, capturing them and then imprisoning them to indulge his sexual whims. Often about at night, he was also perceived as a vampire. He died, it is said after being pursued across the Moors by a pack of black hounds and that, after his death, fiends and hell-hounds held celebrations in the moorland wilderness. There has been some speculation that this local legend was the source of Conan Doyle's inspiration when he wrote *Sherlock Holmes and the Hounds of the Baskervilles.*

When the Squire died, however, the locals were not going to take any chances. Not only did they bury him deep but they covered him with a heavy stone and made a substantial tomb chest. Then to make doubly sure they erected a brick building around the tomb with a stout iron grille on the side facing the church. Some say this is to prevent him getting out, others say that it is to prevent his spirit returning. But one memory lingers on in the locals' minds and that is the reputation that Cabell was a vampire. It is said that if you place your hand through the grille of the grave after the sun has gone down it will be bitten thus sentencing you to eternity as one of the 'undead'.

The tomb is still there behind the grille and will be easily found as it is close to the door of the church. But few villagers venture there after dark. When I visited it with a colleague on a dull January afternoon not only did it look foreboding but the whole church had an air of dereliction. Sadly it had suffered substantial damage from a fire which mysteriously occurred in July 1992. On the chest tomb somebody had thrown a crudely fashioned wooden cross with a pointed end : for protection against the vampire? My sources tell me that the seat of the church fire was the altar but its cause was never fully established. Locals believe it was 'black magic'. The verdict is yours!

South Brent
The Priest's Murder

The next town along the A38 road and the moorland fringe is South Brent. Again my story concerns the church for it has an unenviable record. It is, I believe, the only church in the country, apart from Canterbury Cathedral, where its priest has been murdered whilst taking a service. The church itself dates back almost a thousand years with its tower of Norman origin and the rest dating from the thirteenth century. The terrible crime which I mention occurred over five hundred years ago, in 1436. The vicar was a John Hay and he had just completed *Corpus*

Christi vespers. Suddenly, and for no known reason, a small group led by a local man by the name of Thomas Weke dragged the vicar, dressed in full vestments, from the altar and through a small doorway into the churchyard where he was beaten to death. It is not known what happened to the perpetrators of this heinous crime but one can expect that vengeance was swift.

Another South Brent vicar was deposed from the church. This occurred over two hundred years later during the period of the Civil War when the vicar was a John Gandy. He was turned out by Parliamentary forces but was fortunate enough to return when the Monarchy was restored. Both he and John Hay rest in the churchyard. The doorway through which John Hay is believed to have been taken to his death has long since been blocked up but its outline can still be seen.

Across The Moor
More Hauntings & the Corpse in the Chest

Our journey has now virtually covered the fringe of the Moor so our final drive will be across the centre, from Yelverton to Moretonhampstead, where there are a few more local tales to tell.

The first of these concerns what is now the B3212 road between Two Bridges and Post Bridge, and in particular the stretch where it passes close to Powder Mills and Bellever. There have been a number of stories told of motorists driving past here and experiencing a sensation as though unseen hands had gripped the steering wheels of their vehicles in an attempt to make them crash off the road. In some cases a crash has actually occurred.

Powder Mills, which lies just to the north of the road and is now a pottery, used to be a nineteenth century gunpowder factory, hence its name. But an event said to have happened here in 1924 does have some relevance to the sensations felt by those motorists. Then, it is said, a young woman sleeping there was awakened by a noise she had heard at the window. Looking up, she saw a large hairy hand clawing at the glass as if attempting to get in. Immediately, out of fear, she made the sign of the cross whereupon it vanished.

Further along the road is a very popular meeting place, the Warren House Inn. At over 1400 ft. above sea level not only is it one of the highest buildings on the Moor but is reputed to be the second highest inn in the Country. However, it is not as old as it appears, having been built around a hundred and fifty years ago to replace the New Inn which originally stood on the other side of the road. To the front of the inn, on the open moor, can be seen the long trenches where the tinners used to work whilst nearby were the rabbit warrens which provided their staple form of food. One tradition of the inn which, until recently, was kept going over the years concerns the fire in the bar. Using mainly peat from the moor it was never allowed to die and was reputed to have burnt continuously for over a hundred years.

In winter the Moor can be a very bleak place and the Warren House Inn is no exception, often being cut off from the outside world by snow. One story I heard, but cannot substantiate, concerns a visitor to the Inn many years ago. It was mid-winter and a snow storm was beginning to reach blizzard proportions. A lonely traveller reached the Inn but realised it would be folly to go further. He asked the landlord for accommodation but with this being limited he was offered the spare room which he gratefully accepted. Unpacking his few things, the traveller looked around his new surroundings until his eyes alighted on a large chest in the corner of the room. It was tightly closed but by now his curiosity had got the better of him. Slowly he raised the lid ...

... The landlord was busy downstairs in the bar when the visitor rushed downstairs and burst through the door. His eyes were wide open and at first he babbled incoherently ... there was a body in the chest in his room! The landlord readily agreed but tried to put the guest's mind at rest. It was only father, he explained. As the weather was too bad to get him to church for a funeral he was keeping him in the chest until it got better!

Truth or fiction? I don't know but discussing this with a colleague I was told that he had seen a similar chest at Chagford. That particular one had three locks and was in fact used for the storage of a body when conditions were too bad for a burial. I suppose when you think about it, in the days before mortuaries and Chapels of Rest, they had to keep corpses somewhere so perhaps the story of the Warren House Inn may be true after all. However it does make one think twice about opening strange chests when staying in hotel rooms overnight!

—— Moretonhampstead's Murder ——

About three miles north-east of the Warren House Inn, on the road to Moretonhampstead, is another stretch of highway where, in days gone by, it is said that horses used to rear up as if their bridles had been gripped by unseen hands. Nearby is Beetor Cross, where the B3344 leads off for the village of North Bovey. It was here, at the cross, that the last gibbet to be used on the Moor used to stand. It is often said that animals have a sense beyond the perception of humans so perhaps they felt unease at passing such a site.

Finally we reach Moretonhampstead and the murder of local farmer, Jonathan May, on the 16th May 1835. The circumstances of the murder itself were not unusual. The aftermath, however, seems to have reverberated for over forty years.

The story, as I understand it, was that the victim was robbed on his way home from the White Hart Inn, Moretonhampstead, and his battered body found on the outskirts of the town, near Jacob's Well. He was brought back to the inn where he died without regaining consciousness. Suspicion first fell upon a local man who was later released for lack of evidence. It then turned to two men seen drinking with him. They had, by now, left the area but were traced some months later and brought to Exeter to stand trial. Both were convicted and sentenced to death but one protested his innocence and this was confirmed by the co-accused, a Thomas Oliver. Oliver was executed at Exeter on the 12th August 1836 but evidence was mounting that the other man, an Edmund Galley, had been in Kent at the time of the murder and that there had been a case of mistaken identity. A stay of execution was granted to Galley but it was decided that the judge had given him a fair trial so he was transported to Australia as an alternative to execution. For various reasons the Home Secretary refused to act further on the identification evidence and the campaign for Galley's release continued. Eventually a motion in the House of Commons forced the Home Secretary to act and Galley was pardoned and granted £2000 compensation. By now it was 1879. The slow wheels of justice had taken forty-three years to right the wrong. If that was slow the trial certainly was not. An account in the *Exeter Flying Post,* dated 4th August 1836, extols the virtue that it took so long ... 13¾ hours! Compare that with a modern murder trial which may take many weeks.

Aircrew and Axemen

Walking on Dartmoor can be like walking through Paradise - or Hell. It is an area of ever-changing moods and only the foolish will go unprepared. The Dartmoor Rescue Group is called upon for assistance on many occasions each year. Dartmoor fog is legendary and conditions underfoot can provide the hazardous walking, particularly after heavy rain. There are many stories which can be told about the bottomless Dartmoor bogs!

It is because of these conditions that parts of the Moor are used for military training, particularly by the Royal Marine Commandos. Even the skies above are not immune for these provide the right facilities for low-level sorties by aircraft of the Royal Air Force and Royal Navy.

Over the years the high moors have provided a graveyard for a number of aircraft and their crews and I can recall going to the crash of an R.A.F. trainer near Cadover in 1956. Few sites have reminders but one which comes to mind, which the walker may come across, lies on the track of the Two Moors Way near Hameldown Tor, not far from the prehistoric settlement of Grimspound. This small memorial, set into a granite rock, marks the site where an R.A.F. Hampden bomber, from 49 Squadron, Scampton, Lincolnshire, crashed after being damaged on operations over occupied France from which it was returning on the 22nd March 1941. The four crew members all perished. The memorial also commemorates other aircrew who perished on Dartmoor during World War II.

Driving on the moorland roads is only slightly less hazardous what with 'hairy hands' and sheep and ponies which are completely devoid of any road sense. However many of these roads will lead the visitor to a variety of interesting country pubs. A few have been mentioned already but there are still many which have stories waiting to be told.

I end this chapter, therefore, with a little advice. When drinking at a Dartmoor inn, take a close look at your neighbour - he may not be as innocent as he looks!

Some readers may remember the story of 'Mad Axeman' Mitchell which made the headlines of the national press about twenty years ago. For those who cannot recall the facts they were briefly as follows. Mitchell, an East-ender, was a 'heavy' for one of the big London Gangs and mixed freely with gangland bosses such as the Richardsons and the Krays. As his nickname 'Mad Axeman' suggests he was rather partial to the use of such a weapon as a means of carrying out his 'enforcer' role. Eventually convicted of murder he was sent to Dartmoor to serve his sentence. It seems his reputation preceded him and soon most of the prison lived in terror of him. This included a few of the more junior prison officers who were only too willing to grant a few 'concessions' in return for a peaceful life. One such 'concession' was to allow Mitchell to make unofficial boozing excursions to some of the local pubs. The Elephant's Nest at Horndon was a favourite rendezvous. Apparently this state of affairs lasted for some time before it came to the notice of the prison authorities when, of course, it came to a sudden end.

Mitchell was eventually tempted to make an escape from Dartmoor, aided it is believed by contacts in London's underworld. Unfortunately for him he also had a number of enemies from his shady past and he was to disappear without trace. Those 'in the know' say that he rests peacefully ... encased in concrete under one of our motorway bridges, the victim of a gangland revenge killing.

So, when next sipping your shandy in a Dartmoor pub, look at the man drinking pints next to you. Then ask yourself if the axe leaning against the bar by his side is really for chopping wood ... or has it another purpose. Cheers!

The ruined village of Hallsands

Chapter 5
The South Hams

Yealmpton: *Old Mother Hubbard & The Skeleton*

Newton & Noss: *The R.A.F. & The Ruined Church*

Bigbury on Sea: *Art Deco & Agatha Christie*

Hallsands: *The Force Of The Sea*

Slapton: *The Great Wartime Mystery*

Dartmouth: *Cradle Of Britain's Navy*

Totnes: *The Take-Over Riots*

Berry Pomeroy: *The Most Haunted Castle*

One of the most attractive parts of the County is the South Hams, an area of rolling hills stretching inland from the coast between Dartmouth and Plymouth Sound. It was a part of the County with which I became very familiar when I was posted to Yealmpton in 1962. Leaving the Traffic Department, and Tavistock, behind I arrived in the village at the end of spring. There was one big difference: I now had three stripes on my arm. I didn't know it at the time but I was to witness the end of the era of small rural Police Stations.

———————— Yealmpton ————————
Old Mother Hubbard & The Skeleton in the Pit

Yealmpton sits comfortably on the main road between Plymouth and Kingsbridge and being only seven miles from the former many of its inhabitants found work within the city. The nineteenth century church had a lofty tower and nestled below the main road near the banks of the River Yealm. In the churchyard was a stone pillar which had the name 'Toreus' inscribed on it. It was thought he may have been a Roman chieftain but nobody is certain. Mystery surrounds a phenomenon which is reputed to have occurred there shortly before our arrival in the village, but more of that later.

The police station was almost the last house in the village, strategically located on the main road and next to the Rose and Crown, one of the village's two public houses. A short flight of steps lead to the front door from the pavement. Built about the turn of the century it had a very steep slate roof and exceedingly tall chimneys. Originally it had been the court house and lock-up for the Yealmbridge Petty Sessional Division and evidence of this previous use was only too plain to see for any of its occupants.

Opening the front door the visitor was faced with a long passage which ran straight through the ground floor, from front to rear, except at the far end where there was a kink as it skirted the wide staircase. Entering the police station, the first door on the left was the family's dining room, beyond which was a kitchen tacked on to the side of the house under a lean-to roof. This had a stone sink, wooden draining board, flagstone floor and a field mouse that took up residence in the back of the fridge, presumably because it was warm there! Proceeding further down the passage the next two doors on the left were of heavy steel and had peep-holes - the cells! On the other side of the passage, on the right, the first door was our lounge, the second the section Office and the third the combined bathroom and W.C. The latter was a big room, bigger than either the dining room or lounge. But it had one big drawback. It served not only the Sergeant's family's domestic needs but also police officers working at the station and, occasionally, villagers taken short whilst waiting at the bus stop outside. If the family were taking baths then a queue formed!

Upstairs was also a revelation for this was formerly used as the Magistrates' Court. The main courtroom had been partitioned in two and a false ceiling fitted thus providing two bedrooms of immense size. The small rounded window set high in the front elevation of the house cannot be seen from the inside anymore but was once part of the courtroom. There were a further two bedrooms on the first floor each with black iron fireplaces. Their previous use was easy to ascertain for, although the doors had been painted, the descriptive lettering could still be seen underneath. One read 'Waiting Room' the other, 'Magistrates', that having been their retiring room.

The Yealmpton Section was relatively compact but one which encompassed quite a variety within an area approaching fifty square miles. This included the South Devon coast between the mouths of the Rivers Yealm and Erme. In Yealmpton itself there was a young police constable, usually a probationer, who took lodgings with one of the village shopkeepers. There were four further out-stations, each with a police house and office. These were at Ermington, Holbeton, Newton Ferrers and Brixton.

The Yealmpton Police Station was, despite its interesting past, in poor condition and suffered badly from damp. It would have cost more than the authorities were prepared to pay to make it fully habitable. In view of this preliminary plans were drawn up for a replacement police station to be built on an adjoining site but these were never carried through.

Our second son was born whilst we were there and after a tenure of some two and a half years we were posted to the Divisional H.Q. at Plympton. A Sergeant without a family moved in but did not stay long so I suppose we can say we were the last police 'family' to occupy the house. Yealmpton was closed and the Sergeant's office moved to the fast-growing town of Ivybridge. Within a short space of time all the other police stations in the Section, with the exception of Newton Ferrers, were closed.

Looking back, I think Yealmpton was the happiest posting we had and we made a lot of good friends. Revisiting the village a couple of years ago I saw that the old Police Station, which is now known as 'Peel House', was up for sale. Anyone with £190,000 could have bought it!

On the other side of the road from 'Peel House' is perhaps the South Hams' most photographed building, Old Mother Hubbard's Cottage. It is delightfully picturesque with thick cob walls and a low thatched, billowy roof. It is thought to be at least four hundred years old and there is strong evidence, too, which suggests it was actually the home of 'Old Mother Hubbard' made famous by the nursery rhyme. This was written at the end of the eighteenth century by Sarah Martin who was staying with her brother-in-law, John Pollexfen Bastard, at nearby Kitley at the time. It is said she based the rhyme on the housekeeper at Kitley who retired to the cottage.

Kitley Estate's central feature is its large manor house which dates back to the Elizabethan era, although it has been somewhat altered since. The library used to hold the original first edition of the nursery rhyme. Those readers with a particular sense of humour who watched the popular television comedy, 'The New Statesman', starring Rik Mayall, will know that the central character was an M.P. with the seemingly apt name of Alan Ba'Stard. Kitley has been the home of one branch of the Bastard family since 1710 and has provided Members for a number of Parliaments. I hasten to add that there the resemblance ends!

Another feature of the estate, and open to the public, are the Kitley Caves. Whilst stationed at Yealmpton these were easily accessible and I have visited them on a number of occasions armed only with a torch. Situated in woods near the River Yealm, they are in a particularly delightful spot. Finds of bones belonging to prehistoric man and animals have been discovered there. Since we left the village further excavations have been made and lighting installed, making them a popular venue for visitors.

Crime in the South Hams is, generally speaking, low in comparison with many other areas. There was however one case which was still attracting a lot of interest at the time I arrived at Yealmpton. This was the discovery of a skeleton in an inspection pit on the outskirts of the village. The skeleton was that of a male but the disturbing feature was that the body had been manacled to an iron ring embedded in the side of the pit. Only scraps of clothing remained plus a few oddments from a pocket and a wristwatch. It had been there between fifteen and twenty years. Painstaking enquiries were made for the site had been part of a small military base during World War II and used by sailors operating out of Plymouth. Eventually the skeleton was identified, through the watch, as that of a serviceman but what was never discovered was how, or why, he came to be shackled where he was. That remains a mystery to this day.

A further mystery surrounds the observations made by the vicar of Yealmpton shortly after his arrival in the parish in the 1950s. It was a summer Saturday and his wife was preparing flowers in the church in readiness for the following day's services when he decided to visit her. As he walked along the path on the south side of the church he noticed a hole in front of him. It was about 3 ft. across and he thought it must be due to subsidence. He carried on into the church, spoke to his wife, then thought he would take a second look at the hole. When he returned he could hardly believe his eyes. It had tripled in size. He called his wife out see it as well. Peering in they could see no bottom and dropping a stone they eventually heard it hit stonework. Afraid that persons using the path could be in danger, he decided to get some planks to cover the hole and, in measuring it to determine the length of wood required, found that it was 9 ft. across. On his way back to the vicarage he met the local builder and undertaker, explained to him the problem, and together they returned to the church. Not only was there no sign of the hole but there was no sign of any ground movement at all. It was an occurrence which apparently the vicar, who was quite shaken, did not wish to talk about afterwards so much of the story's substance must have come from the undertaker. He, of course, had not seen the hole himself. He passed on some years ago so it is a story which is difficult to verify although a number of the villagers are still familiar with it today.

Newton & Noss
Old R.A.F. Station and Ruined Church

The busiest area in the Section was the Yealm Estuary with its twin villages of Newton and Noss or, to give them their full names, Newton Ferrers and Noss Mayor. It was always a posting for a senior constable and indeed the holder of the post whilst I was at Yealmpton left soon afterwards to climb the ladder of success. He eventually retired as the Deputy Chief Constable of a large force in the south east of England.

The estuary still ranks highly as an anchorage for yachtsmen and the value of equipment afloat at any one time must amount to millions of pounds. The delightful pubs close to the water's edge at both Newton and Noss are popular ports of call but never caused the police any undue problems. During the war, and indeed for about fifteen years afterwards, the R.A.F. maintained a station, Collaton Cross, on the outskirts of Newton Ferrers. It closed shortly before we left although the married quarters remained for some time after that to house personnel from R.A.F. Mount Batten in Plymouth.

There is another reminder of our need for readiness in war to be found at Noss Mayo. This will be found on the clifftop near Hilsea Point and is shown on some maps as a coastguard lookout. Known as the Gunrow Signal Station it was built in the late eighteenth century, probably around 1795 after the start of the Napoleonic War. Its original purpose was to provide a lookout for checking enemy shipping movements. I understand that, during the World War II, it saw renewed used when the Royal Observer Corps used it for spotting enemy aircraft approaching strategic targets in Plymouth. Since then it has fallen into disrepair.

In another nearby coastal location is the large Stoke Beach camping and caravan site run by the Plymouth Co-operative Society. Its occupancy in summer very nearly doubles the local population but, fortunately, its secluded position is such that it does not detract from the scenic beauty of either the villages or the Yealm estuary. I was a frequent visitor to the camp where, down a steep path, lay the remains of Noss's original fourteenth century church. Today it is very much a ruin. Surrounded by dark trees, and walls covered with ivy, the most common sounds are those of the jackdaws which frequent the crumbling stonework. A number of tombstones dating from the last century and earlier lie forlorn, many marking the graves of fishermen and sailors who were buried here before the new church was built in the village over a hundred and fifty years ago. I have been told that many of those laid to rest here were in fact brought to the cemetery by sea. It can be rather an eerie place, particularly out of the tourist season when all the visitors have gone home and the only sound other than the birds is that of the sea on the rocks nearby.

Taking the coastal footpath eastwards the walker will come

to the private beach at Mothercombe at the mouth of the River Erme whilst, on the other side, is Wonwell Beach. Both can be reached by car although the approach roads are narrow. Bathing can be dangerous at certain states of the tide and a sad reminder of this was the death of Lord Mildmay of Fleet, whose family own the neighbouring estates, when he drowned here in the 1950s. He was a noted steeplechase jockey and one of the big handicap hurdle races is for a cup named after him.

Bigbury
Art Deco & The Agatha Christie Connection

The next estuary is that of the River Avon, not to be confused with the river of the same name upon which Stratford stands. There are immense sands here, too, and once again care with bathing is required. But it is offshore where the interest is to be found. There, a quarter of a mile away across the sands at low tide, stands Burgh Island looking like a miniature St. Michael's Mount. Cut off for about three hours either side of high tide, access is then possible by an ingenious contraption which can best be described as a sea tractor. It carries passengers high out of the water whilst its tracks inch across the hard packed sands below. There are only a couple of buildings on the island and they could not be more diametrically opposed in character.

The Pilchard Inn dates from the fourteenth century and has an atmosphere to match. It is reputed to have been the hideout of a notorious sixteenth century smuggler, Tom Crocker. Tom also had a bit of a reputation as a pirate. A carving reputed to be of him was in the bar the last time I called, together with one of a mutilated excise officer! For a complete contrast, however, one should visit the island's hotel. This large building was erected in the 1920s in true 'Art Deco' style. At the time it became a popular haunt of 'literary' types and Noel Coward was a frequent visitor as was Agatha Christie. In fact she wrote some of her books whilst staying here. More recently a number of T.V. films, where the period has been set in the 1920s, have been shot on location within the hotel and its grounds. However, its exposed position makes upkeep expensive and over the years its fortunes have waxed and waned. Its such an interesting reminder of our more recent past that I hope it remains.

Hallsands
The Force of the Sea

There can be no better reminder of the force of the sea than that which will be found a little further along the coast at Hallsands. On a wintry day, with a high sea running, there is no more 'haunting' spot along this stretch of the shore. Indeed, even in summer, it takes only a little imagination to put yourself in the place of its residents during the storms of 1917. Until then this small village nestled peacefully under the cliffs and provided its inhabitants with a living from fishing the productive Skerries Bank which lies offshore. Their catches of Start Bay crabs and lobster were sought after by many of the fashionable restaurants and hotels.

Then the storms came and the sea was whipped up into heights hitherto unknown within living memory. There was speculation, too, that dredging sand and shingle offshore for building purposes had weakened the village's natural defences. One by one the buildings succumbed to the sea as their inhabitants were quickly evacuated. Today a steep path leads down to what is left of Hallsands. The visitor will find the shells of a few houses, the foundations of their stone walls firmly embedded in rock at the water's edge. There is no sign of human presence. only the sound of the sea and incessant screeching of the gulls.

Slapton
The Great Wartime Mystery

Whilst what happened at Hallsands is no mystery what happened in nearby Start Bay is much more enigmatic. Between Torcross, which about fifteen years ago almost suffered the same fate as Hallsands, and the village of Strete, the main A379 road between Kingsbridge and Dartmouth runs along a shingle ridge. It is a beautiful spot with the sea on one side and a large expanse of fresh water on the other. This is known as Slapton Ley and is internationally known for its wildlife. A field study centre is based here. Roughly halfway along this stretch of road, about a mile inland, is the village of Slapton from which the lake takes its name.

Records on Slapton go back to at least the thirteenth century. During the following century one of its local nobility, Sir Guy de Brien, was standard bearer to King Edward III. In 1373, Sir Guy founded a Chantry in the village, the ruined tower of which still remains. Like so many similar ruins it provokes an 'unreal' air as one looks at the ivy clinging to the walls and watches the jackdaws flitting from perch to perch. To the side of the ruin stands an old inn, aptly called 'The Tower'. It is reputed to have been built as living quarters for the monks employed in building the chantry. It is undoubtedly very old, full of atmosphere, and has one of the best selection of 'real' ales I have found anywhere. Like most old pubs near the coast this one too enjoys a reputation as having been a smugglers' haunt. Somehow in this case I can believe it. Even the seats in the bar are made out of old barrels!

Between 1943–1944 Slapton, together with many of the villages in this part of the South Hams, was evacuated ... lock, stock and barrel. At the time this mass movement of the population was shrouded in secrecy but the reason became evident towards the end of the war. The sands at Slapton were thought to be ideal for the practice of amphibious landings by U.S. Forces in preparation for their ultimate purpose ... the invasion of Europe through the beaches of Normandy. As a result the whole area became a gigantic military camp housing up to 30,000 troops and cut off from the outside world. For a time General Eisenhower set up his Headquarters at Shepley Court, a large house at Blackawton, another of the villages to be evacuated.

It was this massive operation, carried out under a cloak of secrecy, which has left many post-war questions unanswered. Whilst the presence of American troops in the area was not denied, the first film actually showing their training exercises in the area was not released by the U.S. State Department in the Pentagon until 1994. Indeed today on the beach at Slapton stands a large Anglo-American monument commemorating the part played by the U.S. Forces in this theatre of the war. But in the aftermath of the conflict stories began to circulate locally. You may officially evacuate the civil population and enforce an exclusion zone but there will always be those who know ways of circumventing security arrangements ... especially a population with a legacy of smuggling behind them!

Stories began to emerge of a massacre which occurred in April, 1944, whilst practice manoeuvres, code named 'Operation Tiger' were being carried out offshore. A flotilla of fast German E-boats came into the bay and wreaked havoc amongst the unsuspecting Americans. Landing craft, many laden with Sherman or Patten tanks, were quickly destroyed and sent to the bottom of the bay. It was a tremendous blow at the time although , as was proved later, it did not effect the ultimate result of the successful Normandy landings.

That such an attack ever occurred, however, was vehemently denied by both governments for years after the war had ended but the South Hams residents knew better. To find the truth became an obsession and one local businessman in particular was prepared to sink all his finances into this cause. It took years, over thirty to be more exact, before his efforts were rewarded. Initially finding oddments of equipment washed up by the tide, he later put together a diving team which managed to raise from the sea bed one of the tanks which the authorities said had never existed. This tank now stands as a memorial at the end of the beach and close to the car park at Torcross. By now, however, public records were becoming less sensitive and the fact the raid occurred was finally admitted ... but one great secret remained.

In that one attack on the unsuspecting Americans it is estimated that seven hundred and fifty troops lost their lives, an event until recently hushed up by the authorities. Some of the older residents of the area still swear that mass graves were dug in the fields overlooking the Ley and the bodies laid to rest there. This has never been admitted by either government and although the media have also turned their investigative prowess to this facet of the war they, too, have so far failed to find an answer. I asked a friend of mine, who was a police constable at Strete over twenty years ago, what he knew of the incident but he could only reiterate what was said to be 'common knowledge'. He had no views of his own but knew villagers who were 'prepared to swear' they knew what had happened.

As I write this the fiftieth anniversary of that event has passed ... and this one big question still remains unanswered.

Dartmouth
The Cradle of Britain's Navy

The coastal limit of the South Hams is reached at Dartmouth, a superb little town situated on the west bank of the Dart shortly before the river reaches the sea. On the far side is Dartmouth's smaller neighbour, Kingswear, and further north, Torbay.

It's no wonder Dartmouth is known as the 'Cradle of Britain's Navy' for the town is almost dwarfed by H.M.S. Britannia, the Royal Naval College, which overlooks the rooftops from a point high above the river. It is here where virtually all Royal Navy officers are trained, many entering the service direct from school or university as midshipmen. The building has not quite reached its centenary having replaced the earlier *H.M.S. Britannia,* a training ship moored in the river, in 1905.

To adequately trace Dartmouth's maritime heritage would take a book in itself. It certainly dates back to the early days of the Normans when the sheltered anchorage provided a safe haven into which they could bring supplies from their estates in Normandy. There is, however, some evidence that a Saxon settlement was here before that and St. Petrock's Church, near the castle, is thought to have been founded as early as the sixth century.

The port was certainly busy in the twelth century and there are records that in 1147 a fleet of 164 ships set sail from here for the Second Crusade. Forty-three years later King Richard the Lionheart left with another fleet bound for war in the Holy Land. In the reign of Edward III the town sent thirty-one ships to take part in the Siege of Calais during the Hundred Years' War with France. Quite some record, but the biggest fleet ever to sail from the town must have been in 1944. For the thousands of U.S. troops who had been training further along the shore near Slapton the moment of truth had come. No fewer than an estimated 480 ships slipped out of the River Dart bound for the beaches of Normandy. It was 6th June - D-Day.

Unknown to many of the American troops was the fact that, for some, their ancestors may have visited the town before them. It was here that the *Speedwell,* which was accompanying the *Mayflower,* called in 1620 with her Pilgrim Father passengers whilst en route to America. Apparently the ship sprung a leak and they stayed at Dartmouth for eight days whilst repairs were made. Unfortunately it seems that these were not successful and the vessels had to put into Plymouth for a second attempt to rectify the problem. It seems fairly safe to assume that, had the Dartmouth ship-repairers made a better job, then Dartmouth and not Plymouth would have the recognition as their final landfall before reaching the New World.

Protecting the town from the sea has always been a priority for Dartmouth and the sixteenth century castle, built by Henry VIII near the mouth of the River Dart, is a prime example of early British coastal defences. At times of danger a chain would be slung across the river to the smaller castle at Kingswear. In the town itself, at the end of the quay, is a much smaller fortification at Bayard's Cove. This was built by the townspeople themselves around 1510 to house artillery as a secondary line of defence for the harbour.

As one can imagine, there are many tales of smuggling in the area and the earlier inhabitants of Dartmouth would also waste no time in plundering the wreck of any vessel unfortunate enough to be driven ashore. A report from the Inspector of Coastguards at Dartmouth, dated 24th May 1835, graphically describes how between five and six hundred people came from all directions when the Brig *Achor* floundered. He stated that they were "violent in conduct and eager to plunder". It seems the coastguard were greatly overwhelmed because he concludes by reporting that, despite their efforts, much of the cargo was stolen.

Of course, other than the town watchmen or parish-appointed Constables, there was no organised police force in Dartmouth at that time. The first indication we have that things were improving was in 1857 when the Dartmouth Borough Council asked the County to undertake the policing of the Borough with the stipulation that there should always be three resident Constables. A later Chief Constable's Report, showing the disposition of the Devon Constabulary in 1878, confirms that the establishment within Dartmouth Borough was still three constables.

Today big libel actions are frequently in the news, not least because of the celebrities involved and the immense sums of money awarded as damages in some of the cases. Dartmouth, too, has had an interesting libel case although very few will ever have heard of it. Nevertheless it has a place in history because it is believed to be the very first time a Chief Constable has ever sued a newspaper for libel. It occurred in 1888 when Chief Constable Gerald de Courcey Hamilton sued the proprietors of the *Western Daily Mercury*. The matter giving rise to the issue was not of great importance but it was a question of honour. Apparently the paper expressed its regrets and the case was concluded. There is no record of any costs being awarded, the Chief Constable being pleased that his actions had been vindicated.

Totnes
The 'Take-Over' Riots

Totnes, like Dartmouth, is also on the border of the South Hams and stands at the head of the navigable section of the River Dart. Centrally situated quays provide facilities for small coasters bringing cargoes - mainly of timber - to the town as well as embarkation points for the many pleasure craft and ferries plying the river as far as Dartmouth.

There is evidence that the town minted its own coinage as long ago as Saxon times. Traditionally, however, it is much older and in the High Street is the Brutus Stone, said to be the site where Brutus, an ancient Trojan, paused after landing in England for the first time. The Normans later fortified the Saxon settlement by placing a wall around it, parts of which still stand. The best point of access to these ancient ramparts is by stone steps leading up from the High Street near the arch. The Normans also built a castle above the town which has a special place in history as it was one of the very few built never to be involved in conflict. It therefore still stands very largely intact and today is under the care of English Heritage.

Policing in Totnes was undertaken by its own Borough Force until July 1884 when responsibility was taken over by the Devon Constabulary. By all accounts this was not a popular move and by the time the hand-over period arrived at midnight there was an angry crowd of between two and three hundred protesters on the streets. They marched through the town banging tin pots and other utensils and shouting loudly. *The Devon Weekly Times,* publishing details in its edition dated 4th July 1884, reported that the uproar was 'hideous'. The object of their march was to demonstrate their feelings outside the homes of those councillors who had been in favour of the change. One councillor had a substantial number of windows broken. By two o'clock, after singing 'Auld Lang Syne', the crowd dispersed of their own will. This was just as well as the Borough Force had by then ceased to exist and the County presence did not arrive until shortly before noon. It then comprised a Sergeant and two Constables.

Totnes was to grow in importance as a centre of policing and records show that it had divisional headquarters' status prior to 1920. Indeed in a re-organisation held that year, when the number of police divisions were reduced from thirteen to eight, Totnes was one of those to keep its status. This remained until the amalgamation of Police Forces in 1967.

To get some idea of law and order in the Borough in the last century a visit to the Guildhall is recommended. This is situated along the Ramparts' Walk near the Parish Church. I have seen it described as "an odd little building, apparently too small for the town". It certainly has character, tucked away in a quiet corner as it is. It contains the old courtroom which was used until about twenty years ago when the Magistrates' Court moved to new premises on the outskirts of town close to the Police Station. In my earlier years of service I gave evidence here on many occasions. It also contains a council chamber which dates back to the early seventeenth century and a list of Mayors dating back to the 1300s. Now open as a museum, exhibits include stocks, an early man-trap and an old prison cell.

To recreate the atmosphere of an earlier Totnes, once a week during the summer, local traders have dressed in the costumes of their Elizabethan ancestors. Their appearance certainly adds to the local colour.

Berry Pomeroy
The Most Haunted Castle?

Only a couple of miles from Totnes, and right on the fringe of the South Hams, is the small village of Berry Pomeroy. It would be remiss of any writer on the 'unusual' aspects of Devon not to mention the castle which lies on the outskirts of the village and is reputed to be the most haunted in the country. Many booklets have already been written about the castle and its ghosts and these are available either at the castle itself or in the bookshops of neighbouring towns. At the same time, however, I feel a few words are worthy here if only to whet the readers' curiosity enough to make a visit in order to see for oneself.

The approach to the ruined castle is by way of a long drive, at the end of which the castle is set in a strategic position with one side perched on the edge of a cliff. The site has a long history dating back to Norman times although little of the first settlement still remains. For the first five hundred years of recorded history it was the home of the de la Pomerai family who came to Britain with the Norman conquest. In later years their name became anglicised to Pomeroy. It is thought that the first stage of the castle was completed by the early 1300s and it is the ruined wall, tower and gatehouse of this development which still stand today. In the sixteenth century, however, the castle came into the hands of the Seymour family and the Lord Protector Somerset. He had great plans for the site and immediately set about constructing a lavish mansion within the then existing fortifications. Much money was spent and then, quite suddenly, all additional work stopped. The reason for this abrupt change of plan remains a mystery today as, unfortunately, no documentary evidence has been found to provide an explanation. Slowly the Seymour building, too, fell into disrepair and today it adds to the melancholy atmosphere which pervades the site.

One can imagine the legends which have grown up over the years, perhaps the most famous of which relates to the ghost of Lady Margaret de Pomeroy. She and her sister, Lady Eleanor, were both apparently in love with the same man. Margaret was very beautiful but Eleanor was the eldest and very jealous. Fearing she would be the loser in the love battle she imprisoned Margaret in a dungeon beneath one of the towers and allowed her to starve to death. The tower still stands and today is known as Lady Margaret's Tower. A narrow, twisting, stone staircase leads one down into the dark, damp quarters where the unfortunate maiden lived out her last days.

It is said, however, that the spirit of Lady Margaret does not rest peacefully and that, when the occasion calls, her ghost will be seen haunting the ruins. Dressed in a white flowing robe, her long fair hair is said to mask a face which, once beautiful, now carries a tortured look of pain and anguish. She is reputed to be a harbinger of death. Whilst the victim may not be the person who actually sees the apparition, it is said that death will closely follow a member of the family or other associate.

The legend was given some credence many years ago by the story of a local doctor who was called to visit the sick wife of the caretaker at the big house and saw the ghost of Lady Margaret whilst making his house-call. He was not aware of the legend at the time but, noticing how pained she looked and thinking she was a visitor to the house, he remarked on her presence to the caretaker. The poor man immediately became extremely troubled and told the doctor of the legend. An examination of the patient showed she had made a complete recovery and the doctor tried to reassure the caretaker that at least his wife was all right. The next day she was found dead and there was no medical reason why she should have died. An incompetent diagnosis? Maybe, but I think not, particularly if, as it is said, the doctor concerned went on to become Chief Physician to the Prince of Wales of the day, for such posts are not usually filled by incompetents.

Today the castle is in the care of English Heritage. It is a popular site and high on the list for many tourists. As for the locals ... there are very few who would be seen within half a mile of there after dark.

The eerie ruins of Lydwell Chapel where travellers seeking refuge were brutally murdered

Chapter 6
Routes from Exeter

Pinhoe: *The Priest And His Donkey*
Bradninch: *The Roots Of Daniel Boone*
Cullompton: *Day Of the Nine Bloodstained Corpses*
Tiverton: *The Unsolved Murder*
Bickleigh: *Mary Rose & The P.O.W.s*
Bampton: *Pony Fairs & Lethal Icicles*
Black Dog: *The Ghostly Sentinel*
Holcombe Rogus: *The Crying Baby*
Upton Pyne: *Vicar Who Led The Policeman Astray*
Exeter Canal: *The Brave Bobby*
Exminster: *Sad Murder In The Radar Station*
Topsham: *Old Sea Dogs & Lager Boats*
Haldon Hills: *Happy Walks & Horrid Murders*
Chudleigh: *Highwaymen & Haunting Bishops*
Stover: *Little Poland*
Crediton: *The Family Connection*

M y first posting to Headquarters, in the days of the former Devon Constabulary, was as a member of the Traffic Department and our patrol routes radiated from Exeter. However, we did not police the city itself as, until 1966, it had its own Force. In this final chapter, therefore, we look at unusual events and items of interest which can be discovered within relatively short drives from the city but which have not been covered elsewhere.

Pinhoe

The Priest and his Donkey

Now within the city boundary is the village of Pinhoe which, until the nineteen-sixties, was administered by the County Council and had its own police station. The small parish church stands proud on a hill to the north of the village and, usually floodlit at night, provides an attractive sight. It also has an important place in English history with a story which unfolds at the end of the first millennium. Records show that in 1001 A.D. a Danish army invaded Britain, landing a large force at what is now Teignmouth. They sacked the Saxon settlement before setting off inland across the countryside, burning and pillaging other villages as they advanced. By the time they reached Pinhoe a Saxon defensive force under King Ethelred the Unready, was waiting for them and a fierce battle followed. Legend has it that, when the Saxon force were running short of arrows, the priest at Pinhoe crept through the Danish lines with his donkey and returned with a fresh supply thus enabling the defenders to win the battle. In recognition of this brave act, and its contribution to victory, the King awarded the priest, and his successors, an annual pension of one Saxon Mark. This amount was said to represent the cost of feeding one donkey for a year. The allowance is still apparently paid, but to church authorities rather than the vicar personally, and appears in the Government's finances as a charge against the National Debt. Today it bears no relationship to the cost of feeding a donkey as no account has been taken of inflation and it is worth only a few pence.

Bradninch
The Roots of Daniel Boone

Every police officer who has served in Devon will be familiar with 'The Castle' and 'Bradninch Hall' for these were the venues for the principal Courts of the County and are situated in central Exeter. On the occasions when the Crown Court is sitting the presiding Judge· can be seen arriving, and leaving, dressed in judicial regalia and with a police motorcyclist preceding his official limousine. The village of Bradninch, after which the Hall is named, lies on high ground above the valley of the River Culm just north of the main road between Exeter and Cullompton.

Today Bradninch is a quiet place with an appearance which belies its important past. Although now classified as a village it used to be a Borough in its own right with a Mayor who, in importance, ranked above that of neighbouring Exeter. Its charter dates from 1208 although it was in possession of a common seal almost a century before that. The Borough maintained its own police force until 1865 at which time it became part of the County Constabulary. After that prisoners were committed to the county prison instead of the borough gaol. The mayoralty existed until 1886 when it, together with the Borough, was finally ended under the provisions of the Municipal Corporation Act 1883. The village still retains traditional links with the Crown and much of the land in the area is owned by the Prince of Wales as part of the estates belonging to the Duchy of Cornwall. I understand that one of Prince Charles's minor titles is that of Lord of the Honour and Manor of Bradninch.

The fifteenth century church survived the two disastrous fires which destroyed many of the houses in 1665 and again in 1832. Comfort House in Hen Street, with its whitewashed walls and thatched roof, dates from 1681. The parish church is on the American Heritage Trail for its connection with Daniel Boone, and a plaque on the main gate states that Squire Boone, Daniel's father, was baptised there on Christmas day 1696. A further plaque inside the church, flanked by the United States flag and that of the State of Kentucky, records the emigration of the family from Bradninch in 1717 when they left to settle in Pennsylvania. It also pays tribute to Daniel Boone as a "great explorer, trail blazer, woodsman and Indian fighter", acknowledging also his role in founding the State of Kentucky.

Nineteenth century records give a good insight into how local offenders were treated. The charge book found at the old Bradninch police station had several entries of women being whipped for petty larceny but an entry, dated 2nd February 1864, also showed contemporary methods for dealing with absenteeism from work. For absconding himself from service a fifteen-year-old labourer, Abraham Westron, was sentenced to 14 days' hard labour. He was also ordered to pay 6s 6d. in costs or face a further seven days. He opted for the extra hard labour!

Sometimes ridicule was the answer to petty offences and another record in January 1864 shows that a James Williams of Bradninch was committed to six hours in the stocks for drunkenness. It is thought that this is the last time stocks were used in Britain as a form of punishment and they have been preserved in the local Guildhall.

One link with the village's important past still remains and will be found by the banks of the River Culm. This is the paper industry which was founded there at the end of the eighteenth century. Today the mills at Hele and Silverton still produce a wide range of paper goods. In the past one area of specialisation was making paper suitable for banknotes and needless to say the security arrangements were ultra-strict. However, for any potential law-breakers, I recently checked with the Mill concerned and found that such production shifted elsewhere some time ago!

Cullompton

The Day of the Nine Bloodstained Corpses

Only three miles from Bradninch is the town of Cullompton. Prosperous in the past, much of its early wealth was based on the wool industry. One legacy of this era remains at nearby Uffculme where one of the mills has been restored as a working heritage museum. Like many old towns, it suffered disastrously from fires in the past and most of the buildings have been built since the mid-nineteenth century. One exception to this is the Manor Hotel which is situated in the main street and dates from 1600. The narrows of the High Street still cause traffic queues to form despite the fact that the town is now bypassed by the M5.

For years the town maintained a red brick Victorian-style Police Station and Magistrates' Court in the main street although it was vacated some years ago and has had a number of uses since then. The earliest record I can find of a Police Station in the town is in a Chief Constable's report dated June 1857, the year after the Devon Constabulary was formed. In it are details of arrangements made for renting the Police Station at Cullompton and the provision of three cells, quarters for three constables, office for a Superintendent and a petty sessional room. A record made the following year indicated that, after protracted legal arrangements, the purchase of the building was completed. By 1864 Cullompton was a Divisional Headquarters with a Superintendent, two Sergeants, one 1st Class at Cullompton, the other 2nd Class at Bampton and total establishment of nineteen Constables. Whilst the town ceased to be divisional headquarters many years ago, and the court has been shifted to Exeter, Cullompton still maintains an important police presence. The modern police station, situated only a few hundred yards from access to the M5, is the base for traffic officers patrolling a large section of that main highway. They are strategically based for checking all traffic using that route to either enter or leave the force area.

Cullompton is also reputed to be the locality of one of Devon's most horrific murders, albeit an event which occurred during the closing years of the seventeenth century. A former colleague informs me that a few locals can recollect scant details of this infamous crime seemingly committed by one Thomas Austin, a man of wealthy farming stock who became unable to manage the affairs of the prosperous farm he inherited from his parents. Although he married well, and received a substantial sum of money as part of the wedding dowry, it is said he frittered the 'seed corn' away on extravagant living and lavish parties for a new-found circle of friends. Soon he was borrowing money to sustain his now accustomed life-style. But debts have to be repaid and it has been said that he turned, with some initial success, to occasional activities as a highwayman.

It seems that even this pursuit failed to provide sufficient income to satisfy all his creditors. There was, however, another alternative. He had an uncle who lived nearby and it was to his home that Austin went on that fateful day but when he arrived his uncle was out. His aunt, however, greeted him warmly and invited him in to the house where her five children were playing. Suddenly it seems that something snapped in Austin's mind for it has been recorded that he took an axe and cleft it through his aunt's head before setting off after the terrified children, eventually killing them all and piling their lifeless young bodies in a heap. Then, ransacking the house, he found the money he was looking for and returned home.

What happened next is subject to some conjecture but it is likely there was an outburst between him and his wife for soon she, too, lay dead with her throat cut. Two further deaths quickly followed - those of their two children - both of whom were apparently horribly mutilated.

It is reputed that nine bloodstained corpses lay close to Cullompton that day but, as is often the case in the world of crime, fate was to play a hand. Austin's uncle, unaware of events at his own home, had apparently called at the run-down farm for a social visit whilst on his way home. He saw the carnage and his nephew was quickly restrained. From there the law took its course. Retribution in the seventeenth century was swift and soon Austin paid the supreme penalty when he was executed for one of Devon's most heinous crimes.

A completely different but nevertheless interesting case was heard at Cullompton Magistrates' Court in December 1924. This will, I think, illustrate the lingering superstitions country folk have retained over the centuries. The defendant was a man called Matthews who came from the nearby village of Clyst St Lawrence. He had been charged with attacking a neighbour and scratching her with a pin. In his defence he stated that she was a witch and had "ill wished" his pig. He further told the court that she used a crystal ball and insisted that the police should search her house for this evidence. When the Chairman said that witchcraft was a superstitious fallacy which had died out years ago the defendant stoutly refuted these remarks and maintained that it was still being practised locally. The Magistrates were clearly not impressed by the defence and sentenced Matthews to one month's imprisonment. However there are still many in rural areas who would sympathise with Matthews' point of view.

For one final tale about the Cullompton area we return to the present. Those who think that illegal immigrants working as cheap farm labour are mainly a problem for the southern states of the U.S.A., can look closer to home. A swoop by police and immigration officers on a farm at Croyle, near Cullompton, in March 1994, resulted in fourteen persons being arrested on suspicion of working illegally. Of those arrested seven were found to be Poles, one an Ethiopian, one a Czech and the other five Algerians. It seems that the red soil of Devon was being tilled by hands from many lands.

Tiverton
The Unsolved Murder

It is only a short drive by minor roads over the hills to the north-west of Cullompton before Tiverton is reached. This is the largest town in mid-Devon.

Tiverton is an ancient town and is situated at the point where the River Lowman joins the River Exe. The name is derived from the fords which cross both rivers here and is mentioned in the Domesday Book. The castle, set in the town, dates from the thirteenth century and used to be the seat of the Courtenay family, the powerful Earls of Devon. During the civil war, however, it fell to Parliament's army under Fairfax and was partially destroyed so it could be of no further use. The principal feature to survive is the huge gatehouse.

Across town, Blundell's School acquired a good reputation as a seat of learning, and the old building, which dates from 1604, can still be seen. It is said that its roof timber came from ships of the Spanish Armada. It was also used by General Fairfax as a local headquarters during the siege of the castle. The present school moved, however, to much more striking premises on the edge of town in 1882.

The town was devastated by fire in 1731 but fortunately has survived relatively intact since then. For lovers of architecture some fine examples of the Georgian period can be seen today. Some earlier examples remain and of some interest are the town's Nonconformist churches which were endowed by seventeenth century benefactors. The Baptist church dates from 1607 which puts it amongst one of the oldest in the south-west. The Congregational church dates from the same period and had as its first minister the Puritan writer, Theophilus Polwhele, whereas the Methodist Church, as if not to be overshadowed by the other two, ranks John Wesley as one of its founders.

Tiverton has also weathered industrial changes with some degree of luck. It was particularly prosperous between the fourteenth–seventeenth centuries when fortunes were founded on wool. By the end of the eighteenth century, however, the Devonshire woollen industry was failing and the recession was hurting Tiverton the same as everywhere else. Then luck changed. At the beginning of the nineteenth century a Midlands lace maker, one John Heathfield, was concerned by Luddites who were causing damage at Loughborough where he had established his business. As a result he looked for more peaceful pastures and, in 1816, moved to Tiverton where he invented a bobbin machine which revolutionised lace making. Expansion into other fabrics followed and now the local factories send textiles all over the world.

The Police Force in Tiverton can boast that it holds at least one local record. It was the very last of the small Borough, or Town, Forces to be absorbed into the larger County Constabulary, staying independent until 1st January 1943. In the turmoil of war little publicity was given to the fact that the smallest police force in the country had passed into history.

Few records exist concerning early policing in Tiverton but they obviously had insufficient men to deal with Bread Riots which erupted in the town in 1847. Then a contingent of troops was called in from Exeter to assist the Constable and two Special Constables. Later an H.M.I's report on police forces throughout Britain, dated 1867, shows that Tiverton then had an establishment of seven officers. He also reported that the area covered by the Borough was too large to be adequately policed by this number.

The former Borough police's headquarters was originally a debtor's prison which was built in 1844. It was taken over by the police in 1877 and used up until the nineteen-fifties. There was an earlier gaol to the east of the town where the records of one of the inmates shows only too well how harsh Tiverton justice could be at times. Apparently in 1798 a sixty-one year-old local woman was convicted of receiving stolen property and sentenced to fourteen years' transportation to Australia. Then they had second thoughts that because of her age she would not be able to stand up to the long and arduous sea journey. Probation? No way. She served fourteen years in Tiverton prison, finally being released in 1812 at the age of seventy-five.

Inland, rivers normally flow peacefully on their way to the sea. They attract artists, nature lovers and others who appreciate the tranquillity that the rippling of water can bring to the human mind. But rivers can have darker sides, for instance when swollen by floods or their natural harvest becomes the target for poachers.

In the salmon-frequented rivers of Devon poaching has always been a problem and water bailiffs constantly patrol their banks to safeguard the rights of the owners. To fish for salmon legally can be a very expensive pastime but for the poacher there is always a market for his ill-gotten gains. It was this illegal trade which was responsible for Tiverton's only unsolved murder.

Archibald Reed was a thirty-five year-old water bailiff and a family man. He was employed by the Tiverton Fishing Association and described as strong in body and a very conscientious worker. Poaching had been on the increase as a summer drought had reduced water levels but he thought he would have some luck as he had received information that four men would be fishing the river that night. It was Friday, 29th July, 1887, when he left home at about eleven o'clock in the evening, armed only with a stout stick. As he left the house he told his wife not to expect him home until about seven in the morning. She never saw him alive again.

His body was found early next morning by a game-keeper returning home from patrolling Collipriest Woods. These lie back from the east bank of the River Exe just to the south of the town. The body lay in a few inches of water close to the river bank. Reed's throat had been cut so deeply that the head was almost severed. A number of other knife marks had penetrated the face around the eyes. His hands were also badly slashed indicating that he had put up a brave fight and had tried to grab the weapon. His flesh had been literally cut to the bone in the attempt and the ferocity of the attack was such that more than one man must have been involved. Drops of blood led from the scene towards the road to Exeter so it was safe to assume that at least one of the attackers had also been injured.

The trail ran cold and nobody reported seeing any persons with injuries despite a reward of £100 being offered for information. But perhaps the most unfortunate aspect of this case, when viewed in retrospect, was that Archibald Reed had kept all the information to himself. Only he knew the name of his informant and likely identity of his killers. Sadly, that information died with him. The case was never solved.

Bickleigh
Mary Rose and The P.O.W.s

Only a few minutes drive South of Tiverton is the small village of Bickleigh. The village itself is actually by-passed by the main road and therefore rarely visited but the main points of interest are near the bridge which carries the main road over the River Exe. The cottages which lie at the water's edge on the river's west bank are a photographer's dream. In fact they grace the cover of my Ordnance Survey map for the area. On a hillside behind the cottages is one of Devon's earliest vineyards whilst, on the opposite bank of the Exe, is Bickleigh Mill which offers a number of attractions.

Only a short distance from the bridge, and well signed, is Bickleigh Castle. It is actually a manor house which has been fortified and further protected by a moat. Originally dating from the Norman period, it passed into the ownership of the Carew family in the sixteenth century. It was Admiral Sir George Carew who was captain of the *Mary Rose* when she capsized and sank off Portsmouth whilst on her maiden voyage. To mark this connection there is a *Mary Rose* exhibition in the castle.

There is also a smaller, fascinating exhibition centred on equipment used by spies and escaping prisoners of war during World War II. It is reputed to be the most comprehensive collection of its kind and a 'must' for all would-be escapees.

Bampton
Pony Fairs and Lethal Icicles

Six miles North of Tiverton the town of Bampton marked the limit of our patrols from Exeter. Further on, the traffic patrols from Barnstaple took over. Like many towns of similar size, Bampton has lost its status as a Sergeant's station and the former police station has been closed. However one big event occurs in the town which calls for a sizeable police presence and that is the annual Fair which is held towards the end of October. It was originally incorporated by charter in 1258. Although not as big as it once was it nevertheless still attracts thousands of followers, many drawn for the sale of Exmoor ponies. These have roamed the Moors since time immemorial and certainly since there was a Celtic settlement here.

A relic of punishments past will be found near the church tower where the stocks are now situated whilst a reminder that death can come from any angle is made acutely evident on a tablet situated on the wall of the church. This is in memory of a young lad killed by an icicle!

This area, too, has its ghost stories. The one I heard concerns a young girl said to haunt Holwell Farm which is about a mile east of town. She apparently drowned in the River Batherm, near the farm, in the eighteenth century.

Black Dog
The Ghostly Sentinel

The curiously-named village of Black Dog lies in sparsely populated countryside west of Tiverton past such local landmarks as Hangman's Hill Cross and Gibbet Moor Farm. Surprisingly (considering its size), there used to be a Police Station here until about twenty years ago. In fact a friend of mine was the village Constable at one stage of his career but his only claim to fame was being caught drinking in the local pub. Unfortunately he was in full uniform at the time and was seen by the Superintendent who was making one of his exceedingly rare visits.

According to my friend the village gets its name from the black hound which is said to have guarded the entrance to a tunnel which ran from an old well at the village crossroads to Berry Castle. This is the remains of an iron-age settlement about a mile away. The tunnel was used as an escape route during the Civil War and although the dog is still supposed to haunt the village my former colleague was adamant that he had never seen it.

Holcombe Rogus
The Crying Baby

Before we return closer to Exeter I must put on record a ghostly tale from the village of Holcombe Rogus which lies abut three miles North of Junction 27 on the M5 and close to the County boundary. Holcombe Court, an old manor house, has stood in splendid style behind an impressive gatehouse, and close to the church, for nearly five hundred years. For almost four hundred of these, until 1858, it belonged to the Bluett family. According to the legend, soon after the new owners took up residence they were aware that they could, on occasion, hear the faint crying of a child. This continued for some time although there were no other manifestations. Some time later in the course of making some alterations to the house the skeletons of a young woman and a child were found. They were given a Christian burial and the crying duly stopped. The popular legend is that one of the earlier ancestors of the Bluett family, John Bluett, who lived in the manor in the sixteenth century, shut up his mistress and her baby in an attic room and allowed them to starve to death. His motive? It allowed him freedom to marry a wealthy widow.

Upton Pyne
Where the Priest Led the Policeman Astray!

Barely outside the city limits, the village of Upton Pyne lies just north of Exeter on a spur of high ground between the Rivers Creedy and Exe. Again it was one of those small centres of population which, in the past, used to enjoy the services of their own policeman. No doubt the crime rate was kept down and many villages today would love to have their local 'bobby' back again. For the bobby, however, treading the straight and narrow in a country station was not always easy as an extract from Force Orders dated June 27th, 1865, shows. This points out how conflicts of interest can arise. It appears that on the day in question the 2nd Class Constable stationed at Upton Pyne was found guilty of neglecting his duty and of assisting at hay making for the Rector of the Parish. For this transgression he was fined 5s. The report added the rider, "Constables must implicitly obey orders and not allow themselves to be led away by any person whatsoever."

Exeter Canal
The Brave Bobby

From that story of neglect to another one which illustrates only too well the other side of a policeman's call to duty. A marble plaque situated in the hallway at Force Headquarters pays testimony to the gallantry of Charles Tucker, a young police constable aged 22 years, who gave his life on the 5th May, 1876.

The scene was the Exeter Canal, most of which at that time was outside the city limits and policed at various stages of its length by county officers stationed at Alphington, Exminster and Topsham. On the fatal day young P.C. Tucker was handed a warrant for the arrest of a girl who had been charged with theft. As he approached she ran off and jumped into the canal to make good her escape. Unfortunately she could not swim and was quickly in difficulties in the deep water. P.C. Tucker, himself a non-swimmer, did not hesitate to think of his own safety but jumped in to save her. Tragically the attempt was in vain and both drowned. In what was an unprecedented step at that time the Police Committee awarded his parents the sum of £2.11s to cover the cost of the funeral.

Today the canal is a very popular venue for walkers, many making for one or other of the waterside inns which will be found along the towpath. I wonder, however, how many will have heard of P.C. Tucker as they stroll along the peaceful water's edge.

Exminster
Murder in Former R.A.F. Radar Station

It was not far from the canal bank, near the village of Exminster, that an event occurred in 1958 of which I am only too well aware. It happened only a hundred yards or so past the 'Swans' Nest' a very popular inn near the Exminster marshes. The site to which I refer is now the small industrial estate which lies beyond the hump-backed railway bridge and the inn's car park. It was the site of an R.A.F. radar station, and Royal Observer Corps H.Q., during the war and in fact was maintained as such until the mid-1950s. After its closure it passed into private hands and was at first used as a mattress factory.

My story begins with my partner and I returning from patrolling west of Exeter to Headquarters for our lunch-break. Whilst en route we received an emergency call to go to the factory where a shooting had occurred. The information had originated from a railway signalman on the main line who had a terror-stricken woman with him. She had told him that there had been a family argument at their home adjacent to the factory and her son-in-law had shot her husband and then tried to shoot her.

We raced to the scene and the first sight to greet us was the prostrate form of a man lying across the threshold at the front door. Half his face had been blasted away. Miraculously he was still alive but from the nature of his horrific injuries there was little we could do other than radio at once for more assistance and an ambulance. In the meanwhile our priority was to find the gunman before more lives were lost. I would add that there were no armed response teams in those days! My partner and I decided there and then to start searching the immediate vicinity. As I was familiar with interior of the buildings from their R.A.F. days, I opted to search inside whilst my partner took the perimeter. I must admit my adrenaline levels were high but I was not prepared for the sight which struck me as I entered a storage chamber at the end of a passage. There on a mattress lay the lifeless body of a young girl. She could not have been more than three years of age, and her hands clutched a small posy of flowers. Alongside lay a man. I later learned that he was her father. He had turned the shotgun on himself.

My discovery coincided with the arrival of the ambulance so the next stage of events took me to the Royal Devon & Exeter Hospital with the little girl's grandfather. Officially it was to see whether he made any statement which could be construed as a Dying Declaration but I knew it was just a formality. He died shortly after we arrived.

The whole tragic incident had arisen out of a domestic argument concerning the estrangement of the little girl's natural father and the protectiveness of her grandparents. It is a sad fact that the majority of murders arise from similar situations.

Topsham
Old Sea Dogs and Lager Boats

There is an old local saying: "Topsham was a prosperous town when Exeter were but furzy down." Such is the rivalry between Topsham and its much larger neighbour. In fact even today the locals find it difficult to accept the boundary changes which brought them within the Exeter City limits.

It is thought that its special position at the head of the Exe Estuary was used to advantage by the Romans when they brought supplies to their garrison at *Isca Dumnoniorum,* now more commonly known as Exeter! It remained an important port after the Romans left and indeed achieved even further prominence in 1282 when the Countess of Devon built a weir across the River Exe upstream of Topsham and literally stopped all shipping reaching Exeter. Topsham then became Exeter's only port. This situation prevailed for almost three hundred years until, in 1564, work was commenced on building a new ship canal to once again link Exeter to the sea. The project took three years to complete, but Topsham continued to prosper.

In the seventeenth and eighteenth centuries trade links were forged with Holland and many wealthy Dutch merchants built houses here. Many still stand today and their particular style of architecture with gracefully curved gable ends is an interesting feature of this small town which offers many such surprises.

Two reminders of a maritime past, albeit separated by over a century and a half, can be found quite close to each other. The first is a headstone close to the wall of the parish church. This commemorates a local seafarer, Thomas Randle, who was the master-at-arms on *H.M.S. Victory* during the Battle of Trafalgar. He survived and lived in Topsham to a ripe old age.

To find the second take the steps which lead down from the churchyard to a riverside walk at the end of which is the quay. Here is a large warehouse although it is no longer used in connection with the shipping trade. However, until relatively recent times it was used by a world-famous lager company and freighters would regularly moor alongside to discharge cargoes of continental beer for U.K. distribution. This operation ceased when economic factors deemed it more viable to brew the lager in the U.K. under licence. Today the former warehouse is a flourishing antique centre.

Despite this loss of trade Topsham nevertheless maintains a prominent place in the yachting world and a number of boatyards and ships' chandlers do business here. From the end of The Strand, where the road becomes a slipway, there is an uninterrupted view down the Exe estuary as far as Exmouth. This is an area renowned for its birdlife and which, in winter, provides a home for the elusive Avocet.

Haldon Hills

Happy walks & Horrid Murders

West of Exeter and the Exe Estuary lie the Haldon Hills. This range rises steeply on its eastern slope before a more gradual descent to the west. Rising quickly from sea level the hills give the impression that they could be higher than their actual height of just over 800 feet. Motorists whose destination is either Plymouth or Torbay will normally cross them by way of dual carriageways over either Haldon or Telegraph Hill. Each road cuts through the Haldon Forest, a vast area managed by the Forestry Commission and planted with a variety of trees of which fir is the most prominent although beech is common in some parts.

Here the Forestry Commission provides a number of forest trails some of which, such as the Birds of Prey walk, have a specific purpose. One of Devon's two principal racecourses is situated at the top of Haldon Hill and it is here that the Devon & Exeter Meetings are held.

As well as being a natural landmark in its own right, Haldon provides two others which are distinctly man-made. The most prominent of these, Lawrence Castle, is better-known locally as Haldon Belvedere. This is not strictly a castle at all but an eighteenth century folly built in the shape of a single triangular tower with a castellated parapet at the top. It adds another 70 feet to the highest part of the hills. It was built in 1788 by Sir Robert Palk in memory of his benefactor, Major General Stringer Lawrence who was known as the 'Father of the Indian Army' and who died in 1775. A steep descent from the tower brings one to the village of Dunchideock. It is here that the legendary Devon Treacle Mines will be found. For further information ask the landlord of one of the nearby pubs!

The second man-made landmark lies towards the southern end of the hills. Today, surrounded by trees, it is not so evident from a distance although trails lead from car parks through the forest. I refer to the Mamhead Obelisk. This was erected in 1742 by Thomas Ball, a wealthy landowner who had inherited the Mamhead Estate. It apparently served two purposes. The first objective was as a safety mark for shipping using the 'Port of Exon'. The second was as an ornament for the park surrounding his house.

The Haldon Hills are popular with walkers, and every weekend will find cars in the various car parks as their drivers and passengers go 'walkabout'. Apart from coming across the various view-points the walker can never be sure what else he or she may find. Indeed Haldon played a part in two of the most interesting crimes in recent years.

Here we recall the case of the murder in Budleigh Salterton of millionaire's wife, Juliet Rowe, which was mentioned in Chapter One. The final link in the chain was discovered hidden on the wooded slopes of Haldon. The murder trail had grown cold although officially the file was never closed. The big break came years later when a former employee of Rowe kidnapped a wealthy Surrey businessman. A ransom demand was made and in the meanwhile the victim was kept gagged and bound to a tree in a secluded part of Haldon Forest. He was later found barely alive. Good police work led to the arrest of Keith Rose and it was then that a .22 pistol was found amongst his possessions. Bearing in mind that a similar weapon had been used in the Rowe case, ballistics tests were carried out which showed that it had indeed been the gun used in the murder. A motive for the crime began to emerge: it could have been a kidnap attempt which had gone horribly wrong … maybe Mrs Rowe had recognised her kidnapper as a former employee of her husband. Rose denied the murder but was convicted of it.

The second case, in 1983, was much more grisly and, again, concerned murder. The murder was actually committed in West Wickham but the aftermath certainly concerned local officers. It was, more or less, a domestic affair and concerned a member of a well-known family, Michael Telling, and his attractive American born wife, Monica, with whom he was deeply in love. Sadly, this was not altogether reciprocated and it was alleged she used to taunt him on his prowess as a lover, amongst other things. Finally he could take no more and he blasted her with a shotgun, killing her instantly. Now filled with remorse, Telling could not bear losing his wife so decided to keep her body in an outhouse at their home. About six months later, however, he changed his mind and decided to dispose of it. The site he chose was close to a motorists' view-point above the wooded slopes of the Haldon Hills. But there was a bizarre twist. He still could not bring himself to lose her altogether so, before leaving the body, he decapitated it. One can imagine, therefore, the horror of the poor motorist who found the headless corpse. There was little of the body to identify other than some clothing. Screening this on T.V. brought a response and the net closed in on Telling. He was arrested and his car was searched by police officers. In the boot was the missing head! Even at that stage Telling had been unable to part with it. At a subsequent hearing at Crown Court Telling was found not guilty of murder but guilty of manslaughter due to diminished responsibility.

A continuation of the Haldon Hills, as they extend southwards towards Teignmouth and the Teign Estuary, is known as Little Haldon. Teignmouth golf course is here, and it is the site of one of Devon's earliest airfields.

Haldon Aerodrome operated for fifteen years, between 1929 and 1946. It its early days it was little more than a field but it prospered during the 1930s and was an annual venue for the legendary Alan Cobham Flying Circus. It was also used for a while by the locally-based Provincial Airways. This small airline had also used the airfield at Denbury, near Newton Abbot. After the outbreak of the World War II Haldon Aerodrome was taken over by the Royal Navy and designated as H.M.S. Heron II, a satellite of R.N.A.S. Yeovilton. It was then extended and during the war a number of different types of aircraft operated from there. These included Blackburn Skuas and Boulton Paul Defiants, examples of which unfortunately no longer exist. I understand, too, that it was an emergency landing site for the U.S.A.F. Liberators based at Dunkeswell, being strategically placed as the first landing point on return from maritime patrols.

War over, there was no further use for the site. Civil aviation had already switched to the much better facilities provided by the modern airport at Exeter. Gradually Haldon Aerodrome returned to its natural state and today is overgrown with little trace left of its former use. Unfortunately for today's private flyers, however, the Hills still provide an aviation hazard. Rising steeply so close to the sea, an aircraft making for Exeter and flying too low in very poor visibility runs the risk of flying into them. One such disaster occurred in 1993 when a light aircraft flew in from the Channel Islands in thick fog, and crashed into the forested slopes, killing all occupants.

The site of the former aerodrome was very close to Teignmouth golf course and the aviators' club house was within a couple of hundred yards of the crossroads which lead to Luton and Bishopsteignton. It was at these same crossroads where, in the eighteenth century, the gibbet used to stand and it was here, in 1783, that Games Greenslade was hanged for the murder of the Rev. Gilbert Yarde of Teigngrace. I understand that the body was left hanging there for two weeks before being buried nearby.

For yet another story of evil one does not have to move far from this spot. On the opposite side of the main road from the golf course a track leads down the steep slopes of Little Haldon to woods lying deep in the valley below. Hidden amongst the dark trees, close to a small stream which eventually flows into Dawlish Water, are the remains of the little chapel of Lydwell. It is believed to have been built on what was originally a pagan site and dates from at least the fourteenth century and maybe earlier. It was dedicated to Our Lady of the Well, the well being close to the stream. I must admit I have searched the site on two or three occasions and although I found it dark, dank and rather foreboding so far the well has remained hidden from me. However that is not to say it did not exist for even today much water seeps from the ground around the ruined chapel. It is the well which is the central focus of this story which it is said emanates from church records kept during the period of Bishop Grandisson in the fourteenth century. An entry refers to the Hermit Monk of Lidwell, otherwise known as Robert de Middlecote. Apparently he was purged for crimes committed at the chapel where it is said he robbed and then murdered travellers who sought overnight refuge. He then disposed of their bodies by dropping them down the well. The legend continues that an examination of the well many years later revealed human bones, and stories persist that the spirits of those who were slain still haunt the ruins. The evil monk was subsequently executed for his crimes. Later records indicate that the chapel continued in use until at least the beginning of the fifteenth century but today only one wall with an archway remains substantially intact.

Chudleigh

Highwaymen's Hideaway & A Haunting Bishop

Dropping down the western slopes of Haldon on the A38, a detour can be made from the dual-carriageway into the small town of Chudleigh. In doing so the 'Highwayman's Haunt' will be seen lying back on the left of the road, its entrance 'guarded' by an old cider press. Now a popular inn and licensed restaurant, this is a real 'olde-worlde' building with white-washed walls fashioned from cob and a thick thatch roof. Years ago it used to be known as Rowell's Farm and according to local legend was the hide-out of the popular Chudleigh highwayman, Jack Withrington. His 'beat' was the stage route between Exeter and Plymouth. His four brothers also plied the same trade and eventually all five members of the family paid the same penalty when they were caught, tried and hanged.

In the main street, almost opposite the church, stands what is believed to be Chudleigh's oldest building, the 'Bishop Lacy Inn'. Parts of it date from the fourteenth century when Bishop Lacy was Bishop of Exeter and used it as a summer retreat. It has a reputation for being haunted by a ghost dressed in the garb of a cleric, whom it is believed by some to be Bishop Lacy himself. A colleague of mine, who became a senior detective, was actually born in the pub but even he was unable to provide evidence of a supernatural existence!

Further along the main road is the town's Police Station and a turning here leads to Chudleigh Rocks. This is a large outcrop of limestone which is partially hidden by trees. Nevertheless if you find it there are a number of rewarding walks to be had although care should be taken as some are a little hazardous. It is also here where Chudleigh Cave will be found. I explored part of it many years ago but it is no longer open to the public. I have heard two reasons for this, one being that it has become too dangerous for casual visitors and the other that it is now home to a colony of an endangered species of bat. Either reason seems equally valid but should not detract from the historic interest that, within the cave, remains have been found both of prehistoric man and early animals.

Stover
Little Poland

Beyond Chudleigh, at the Drumbridges Roundabout, one road leads to Newton Abbot. This route also leads to the turning for Trago Mills, an extensive out-of-town shopping complex. A small roundabout controls the junction and, if using this route, note the entrance at the commencement of the private road leading to the shopping centre. It leads into a private estate managed by Her Majesty's Government.

Once known officially as Stover Camp it became more affectionately nicknamed 'Little Poland.' Originally it was built as an American military hospital to take casualties after the Normandy landings but later, after the war, it was used to house Polish refugees. It its heyday, in the twenty years following the war, it was home to literally hundreds of Polish citizens who were unable to return to their native land because of the Russian occupation and, later, their own communist regime. The British Government provided funds for running the camp with administration being undertaken by the then Social Services. Nevertheless the refugees managed many of their own internal affairs and the majority of the older ones had no desire to integrate into the outside world. For many, Polish remained the only language they ever spoke and understood. During this early period to drive past Stover was like driving in Eastern Europe. Peasant women, hunched under massive headscarves, were a frequent sight as they pulled their home-made handcarts along the road whilst scavenging for wood and foodstuff for their pet animals.

For the police the only problem was an administrative one. Officially the Polish residents were registered as 'aliens' and this meant records had to be kept. The file on Poles was larger than all other nationalities put together. Times have changed and the war has been over for half a century. Most of the original occupants of 'Little Poland' have passed away. I believe a few remain. For them Devon is Poland and that is home.

Crediton
A Family Connection

I left Crediton to last although in one respect this town, eight miles north of Exeter and on the scenic route to Barnstaple, is perhaps where I should have begun. There are few early records of policing here but one of the first, a minute to Quarter Sessions in 1855, refers to riots in the town the previous year during which a number of properties were damaged. Legally, once the Riot Act has been read before the mob, the cost of any subsequent damage must be borne by the police authority. It appears that on this occasion a number of local residents were reimbursed a total sum of £8.19s.8d, this money later being recovered by a precept on the local rates.

Two years later, in 1857, a further minute from Quarter Sessions ordered the Force to provide the following accommodation at Crediton ... two cells, a petty sessional court room and quarters for one Sergeant and three Constables. The following year the first steps were taken to purchase a suitable site for the new police station at a cost of £160.

William Mogridge had joined the Devon Constabulary in 1885 and was posted to Crediton in 1902 as the town's Sergeant, a post he occupied until he retired from the force in October 1910. On retirement an elaborate scroll, illuminated in gold leaf, was presented to him by the 'worthies' of Crediton to mark " the esteem and regard for the thoroughly conscientious and efficient manner in which you discharged your duties during the eight years in which you held the position of Sergeant of the Crediton Petty Sessional Division." The scroll is now in the keeping of the Force Museum. I mention it only because William Mogridge was my great-grandfather.

At the turn of the century one of the young Constables at Crediton was a William Holloway. He married the Sergeant's daughter! Which brings me to a fitting end ... or perhaps the beginning!

It is perhaps a good point to stop and turn the car for home. A journey through Devon can provide many surprises. It has the sea and the high moors, the countryside and the towns. It has a heritage second to none and a wealth of folklore and legends to tell, and retell, by a warming winter fire. You could live to be a hundred and still not uncover all there is to know but I hope that in the short period it takes to read this book you will have learnt something new by the time this, the last page, is reached.

Acknowledgements

The contents of this book have come from many sources.

I am indebted to those many colleagues who served with me in the former Devon Constabulary, and latterly the Devon & Cornwall Constabulary, for providing me with so much suitable material. This came not only from fellow police officers but members of the civilian support staff and the Special Constabulary.

I owe a debt, too, to the late Walter Hutchings, a Superintendent of the former Devon Constabulary, who wrote a history of that Force which was published in 1956 under the title *Out of the Blue*. His research into early Force records was used as the source for some of the historical data used in this publication.

Gratitude must go also to those libraries and records offices where the Staff went out of their way to provide extra material from archives.

Other Peninsula Press titles include:

The Secret of the Babbacombe Murder - Mike Holgate
A Glimpse of Dartmoor Prison - Trevor James
A Glimpse of Dartmoor Folklore - Belinda Whitworth
Haunted Dartmoor - R.W.Bamberg
Walking the Stories and Legends of Dartmoor - Michael Bennie
The Witchcraft and Folklore of Dartmoor - Ruth E.St.Leger Gordon

A complete illustrated list of Peninsula Press titles
is available from:
P.O.Box 31
Newton Abbot
Devon TQ12 5XH
Tel & Fax: 01803 875875